# Empowering People

# People

■

## AILEEN MITCHELL STEWART

PITMAN PUBLISHING

*The Institute of Management (IM) is at the forefront of management development and best management practice. The Institute embraces all levels of management from students to chief executives. It provides a unique portfolio of services for all managers, enabling them to develop skills and achieve management excellence. If you would like to hear more about the benefits of membership, please write to Department P, Institute of Management, Cottingham Road, Corby NN17 1TT. This series is commissioned by the Institute of Management Foundation.*

PITMAN PUBLISHING
128 Long Acre London WC2E 9AN

A Division of Pearson Professional Limited

First published in Great Britain 1994

© Aileen Mitchell Stewart

A CIP catalogue record for this book can be obtained
from the British Library.

ISBN 0 273 60344 2 (Paper back)
ISBN 0 273 60745 6 (Cased)

7 9 10 8 6

Photoset in Linotron Century Schoolbook by
Northern Phototypesetting Co. Ltd., Bolton
Printed and bound in Great Britain
by Bell and Bain Ltd., Glasgow

# Contents

■

# Preface

■

Suppose someone offered you a magic spell which could

- increase the performance standards of your staff
- give you more time at work to set strategy and plan developments (instead of fire-fighting and day-to-day coping)
- improve the service you give to your customers (whether outside or inside the organisation)

and then told you the cost: nothing at all! Would you turn the offer down? I doubt it.

Then suppose you were told that this 'magic spell' would cost you nothing to use because you already own it and could use it at any time you liked. Wouldn't you want to cast the spell immediately?

Yet, if you are a manager (no matter what your level in your organisation) you actually *do* possess just such a 'magic spell' but the chances are that you have never used it. Why? Probably because you didn't realise you could.

This 'magic spell' is called empowerment. Empowerment is a very special kind of magic. It actually increases a manager's success by giving power to other people. This book will help you to discover the 'magic' power you already have so that you can use it to transform the way you and your staff work. It offers no miracles, but it will show you a way that you can achieve better results than you thought possible – if you are willing to try.

## 1

# Power and empowerment

**W**hen managers begin to think about empowering their organisation or department, they may also begin to think about the nature of power itself, and how this relates to or differs from authority. They may start to wonder about the consequences for themselves of empowering others. Does empowering others mean giving up one's own power? Does it mean that managers no longer have authority over their staff? We tend to use the words authority and power as if they were interchangeable, seldom stopping to consider the differences between them. Yet it is important that managers do understand the distinction between the two (and other matters besides) if mistakes are to be avoided and empowerment is to work.

The most urgent concern which managers have related to power and authority is the fear that empowering others will weaken their own position and their ability to ensure that targets are met and standards maintained. Accustomed to rule-based systems they worry that if the rules are whittled away then efficiency will dwindle too. These are important and valid concerns so we will look at these sorts of question first.

## Authority

One useful definition of authority stresses that it is essentially a right, specifically the right to decide and command. So a parent has the right to decide that it is a child's bedtime, and to 'command' the child to go to bed. But whether parents always have the power to make this happen on command is another issue entirely! We'll consider the issue of power shortly.

This definition of authority, however, is not the whole story. There is an important distinction between being *in* authority and being *an* authority. The former case is the situation described above, where one occupies a particular role (in this case that of a parent) which brings with it the right to make certain decisions (such as when a child should go to bed) and to command that an instruction ('Go to bed now') is obeyed. But, to extend the example, few parents would consider themselves to be experts on the sleeping habits of children in general, or to be qualified to give professional advice on how to cure sleeping problems in children. If parents want that kind of advice they turn to someone who is *an* authority.

This is an important distinction. Older styles of management relied largely on the manager being *in* authority to get things done. The manager made the rules and the staff's duty was simply to obey them to the best of their ability. But such an approach is clearly unlikely to result in much initiative on the part of staff. It is an approach which is well suited to bureaucracies but is much less effective and suitable in organisations which need to be rather lighter on their feet in response to changing circumstances and markets: exactly the situation facing most organisations today.

Empowerment seeks to eliminate all the unnecessary rules, pro-cedures, standing orders, etc. which actually stand between the organisation and its goals. The aim is to remove as many restric-tions as possible in order to unblock the organisation and the people who work in it, liberating them from unnecessary limita-tions which slow their responses and constrain their action. Empowerment, therefore, will inevitably result in a certain amount of loss of being *in* authority. However, a manager who is *an* authority is a different matter entirely. A manager who is *an* authority has the necessary knowledge and experience to guide and advise staff, helping them to make their own decisions based on that guidance. Such a manager is able to ensure that staff in the organisation or department act appropriately without having to make long lists of rules for them to stick to, or lay down strict orders. The manager who is *an* authority is able to support staff rather than command them. This kind of authority is not lost as a result of empowering staff. It is, in fact, a prerequisite of effective empowerment.

So empowering others may entail, to a certain extent, giving up being *in* authority. True empowerment operates with as few rules as possible. However, the need for some basic, simple rules will always remain. Staff need to know, for example, the boundaries of their discretion if they are to feel truly free to act within those boundaries. And any rules will, of course, always require a certain amount of policing to make sure that they are complied with. Moreover, any loss of being *in* authority due to a reduction in rules and regulations will be more than compensated for by the developing role of being *an* authority. Staff need proper guidance and support if they are to exercise their new power sensibly and appropriately. The empowering manager needs to be *an* authority to whom staff can turn for counsel and suggestions as to how they might best deal with a given situation.

3

Overall, then, empowerment results not so much in the loss of authority over staff as in the exercise of a different kind of authority, generally of a much more satisfying kind.

# Power

Where authority is essentially a right, power, on the other hand, is basically an ability: the ability to make something happen (or prevent it from happening). In the example above, parents can easily exercise this power over a small child by the simple expedient of picking up the child and carrying it to bed. That kind of physical power, however, tends to wane as the child gets older. Then other types of power need to come into play.

## TYPES OF POWER

On the whole managers exercise just three basic types of power: role, expert and resource power. Each of these has its own uses, benefits and drawbacks.

### Role power

Role power is the ability to invoke sanctions against those who do not comply with your commands. It's an effective way to achieve quick compliance in certain kinds of situations. This is the kind of power exercised by the parent who persuades the child to go to bed 'because I say so'. As all parents know, this type of power tends to wane as children grow older and more able to think for themselves. They begin to question whether the mere position of parent is enough to justify issuing commands. They increasingly demand explanations as well as orders, and learn to challenge the explanations if they don't seem to amount to a good reason to obey. Sensible parents regard this as a healthy (if irritating) development. Children need to learn to think for themselves. The first step towards setting their own sensible and necessary rules is learning to query rules set by others. That's how they learn that rules are not merely arbitrary and that some are actually necessary for safety, and so on.

So why do some managers still try to exercise this kind of 'because I say so' power over perfectly mature and intelligent adults at work? There *may* be occasions where its exercise is necessary, though such situations are rare. On the whole, the use of this type of power in management is appropriate only at times of urgent crisis or emergency. So why do so many managers persist in adopting it as their main style? Perhaps because they don't see their staff as mature, intelligent adults but as potentially naughty young children who have to be kept under control. Such managers will never be able to harness the full range of skills that their staff possess. The habitual exercise of role power is not the way to successful empowerment of others.

## Expert power

Expert power, on the other hand, is similar to being an authority: it is based on possessing particular skill or knowledge. It is by using this skill or knowledge that the manager exercises power. Actually, management skills and knowledge are themselves the prime source of such power in most organisations. The manager who is trained and knowledgeable about management issues, and who can exercise a range of management skills and techniques, is in a much better position to make something happen – to exercise management power – than someone without such skills or knowledge.

Actually, if a manager wishes to empower staff, it is essential to exercise this kind of power. Proper use of expert power will enable the empowering manager to plan, implement and monitor the process of empowerment effectively, thus ensuring its success. Without such skill-based power the project would fail. Far from resulting in a loss of this type of power, empowerment depends on it for successful implementation.

There is, however, another important aspect to expert power. The manager who truly wishes to empower staff will try to ensure that they, too, have sufficient knowledge and skill to exercise devolved power successfully. This has obvious implications for training and staff development. But it may also require the empowering manager to be willing to share some of his or her own expertise and knowledge with others. Knowledge, it is often said, is power. If power is to be shared then knowledge must be shared too. The manager who is afraid of sharing knowledge or information will never be able to empower staff. Similarly, it may be important to find ways to encourage and help staff to share their knowledge with one another. In a truly empowered organisation knowledge is a shared commodity.

## Resource power

The third kind of power exercised by managers is resource power: the ability to supply or withhold resources. This kind of power is clearly central to any manager's role. It is also an important aspect of empowerment. No one can hope to empower staff unless they also provide the necessary resources to support that empowerment. One of the first things that must be done is to try to identify the money, expertise, materials, time, etc., which will be needed if empowerment is to be successful. This will probably require the manager to devolve some of his or her own resources along with the power to use them. This will require the careful negotiation, setting and allocation of budgets as well as setting targets for their use.

## Power-role changes in empowerment

It can be seen, then, that empowerment results not so much in the loss of power as in changes in the way it is operated. It requires the enlargement of some authority and power roles as well as increased flexibility over how – and by whom – these roles will be exercised. Empowerment doesn't mean simply abdicating responsibility for what goes on in your team, department, division or organisation. Rather, it means finding the right balance of loose v. tight management structures and controls.

So there is little need to fear losing authority or power through empowerment. Indeed it can be said that a manager needs to be able to exercise the right kind of authority in order to empower others. It might also be said that, in essence, empowerment is simply the effective use of a manager's authority.

# Empowerment

So what is empowerment all about, in practice? And what are its benefits? Empowerment is, quite simply, a highly practical and productive way to get the best from yourself and your staff. It goes beyond delegation to place real power where it can be used most effectively: close to the customer. This means devolving not just tasks but decision-making and full responsibility too.

## Close to the customer

Which people – in most organisations – are closest to the customers? The managers or their staff? The answer is obvious: the staff who deal with them on a day-to-day basis. Yet which group traditionally has least say in how the organisation operates? The answer is usually the same.

Why is this? Because – despite the rhetoric – most organisations don't value their staff quite as much as they claim. They don't truly respect them as fully functioning intelligent adults or trust them to exercise their own judgement outside a set of highly restrictive parameters. They are more concerned to restrict and control staff endeavour than to enable and support it. This may be because managers are afraid of losing control: of staff; of budgets; of projects; of standards. The idea of empowerment worries them because it seems to entail the loss of all that carefully planned control. However, empowerment is not about losing control, but about giving it away.

There's a substantial difference between losing control, and giving it up. Giving up control – empowerment – requires careful preparation and planning. Paradoxically giving control away through empowerment can result in better control over outcomes in the long run. That's because control hasn't ceased to exist; it is simply being exercised by other people: your staff.

So empowerment is not about loss of control, or any other kind of loss either. In fact it's about gain: gain of time, quality, commitment, ideas, etc. Most of all it's about gaining access to the fullest possible range of staff skills and knowledge.

# Staff as a resource

Many organisations continue merely to pay lip service to the much-voiced claim that 'staff are our most important resource'. Attempts to convince staff (and the managers themselves) of this frequently stop at incentive or staff welfare schemes. These are fine, of course, as far as they go. They just don't go far enough. Most such activities are designed to *conserve* human resources – holding on to existing staff or attracting new ones – rather than to *use* them most efficiently and effectively.

Such an approach treats staff as a costly resource, not a valuable one, and fails to recognise the waste inherent in not harnessing the fullest possible range of their skills and abilities. So much for staff as 'our most valuable resource': perhaps a more truthful statement would be that 'our staff are our most under-utilised resource'.

Nor – whatever they may claim – do most organisations really regard the customer as king. Many persist in believing that the only people who really know what the customer needs and wants are the people who see least of them: the senior management team. This is true even of internal customers: the people within your organisation to whom you and your staff supply goods, information or services. Your staff are almost certainly much closer to them than you are. Yet who makes the rules and decisions? Yes, you consult your staff – of course you do. But do you actually empower them to manage their relationships with customers as they see fit, using their own initiative and close understanding of customer expectations and requirements?

Many organisations fail to recognise – let alone harness and use – the knowledge and understanding that even quite junior or low-level staff have about customers and their needs. They prefer to beset people with rules and procedures which are expressly designed to prevent them using their own initiative to provide the customers with what they need. In the end, staff come to rely rigidly on these rules and procedures even where it would seem obvious that they should exercise a degree of discretion. This not only results in poor customer service, but is ultimately very demoralising for staff.

I recently took my family to a local sports centre for a swim. My eldest daughter had just come back from an interview for a place on a training course for unemployed people. I expected that she would be eligible for the concessionary rates which sports centres and the like commonly offer to the unemployed, the elderly, etc. Unfortunately, she had forgotten to bring her unemployment benefit card (the UB40) or her benefit book – the two usual ways to 'prove' that you are unemployed. She did, however, have with her a signed letter from her local Job Centre certifying that she was eligible for the training programme, and a leaflet about the scheme which made it clear that it was for the unemployed only. These she showed to the woman on the till, explaining what they were. The woman flatly refused to accept these as proof of unemployment, on the grounds that she was allowed to accept only UB40s or benefit books. My daughter and I patiently explained yet again that the documents she had in her hand could only belong to an unemployed person. She rebuffed our claim with the charge that though this might be true, she had no means of knowing that they actually belonged to my daughter. We counter-attacked by pointing out that she would have no way of telling whether a benefit book or UB40 belonged to the person showing them either, since anyone could steal or borrow those too. There was, we said, no difference between them in terms of their ability to certify ownership or unemployed status. Cornered and facing defeat, she resorted to the only avenue left to her: tactical retreat. She left (with bad grace) to consult a colleague. We watched them in close discussion for several minutes. She returned. No, she said, with an air of final triumph, she was allowed to accept only a UB40 or benefit book. It was we, therefore, who were finally forced to accept defeat.

What was the result of this frustrating encounter? She had saved her organisation less than a pound but risked losing a future customer. It will be a long time before we go there again, particularly since this was the second such incident there in as many weeks. The same sports centre runs a snack bar selling burgers and the like. A couple of weeks earlier my son and younger daughter had been promised a burger as a treat after their swim. The corridor from the pool to the snack bar was plastered with posters advertising their cheese-and-bacon burgers. The children, as children will, were persuaded by these bright adverts to want a cheese-and-bacon burger. It was not to be. Sorry, said the snack bar assistant, they couldn't have one because she had run out of bacon several days ago. Not so dreadful, you might say, except that the sports centre is only about a hundred yards from a major supermarket.

But the staff of the sports centre are not entirely to blame. Treating people like automata is no way to ensure good customer service. Nor is it any way to win staff's dedication and attention to the job. If you treat people like half-humans you shouldn't be surprised if you only gain – at best – half their commitment and a much smaller fraction of their interest and energy. Small wonder, then, if staff come to seem apathetic and lacking in drive. In an empowered organisation the staff might have felt safe enough to apply a little common sense and initiative in such situations. The woman on the swimming-pool till might have applied her intelligence to deduce that what she was offered was substantially the same as the rules required. The snack bar assistant might have realised that it was better to use some of the till money (leaving an appropriate note and receipt) to buy some bacon than to turn away custom. At the very least she could have removed the adverts promoting this unavailable product. (She hadn't taken down the posters because, she said, that was not her job.)

Why didn't they do any of these things? Because no one had told them that they could – and should. She and her colleague on the swimming-pool till knew the rules and stuck to them. What they didn't do is serve the customer or enhance the business. They defined their responsibilities narrowly in terms of following procedures and rules. They were more afraid of breaking the rules than of turning away custom. It presumably didn't occur to either

10

of them – because, one imagines, they had never been told – that their primary task was to ensure that customers were so happy and pleased with their experience of the sports centre that they would return time and time again. And if that meant bending or breaking some rules in a sensible way in order to reach this prior objective then so be it. In short, they didn't really understand what their job was, or how it related to corporate goals and objectives.

How many other customers had they turned away or alienated between them that month, one wonders. I don't know – neither, probably, does their manager. That's the danger of *not* empowering: you may never know how much business you have lost.

## Staff calibre

But are most ordinary staff, such as those working at the sports centre, able to cope with empowerment, you may ask. Could the average person cope with the additional demands that empowerment would make on them? Well, let's ask another question first. Could you handle more power or responsibility than you currently have, or are you operating at (or close to) the limits of your skill, knowledge, intelligence and experience?

Almost everyone (unless very new to a job) will say that they are by no means at the limit of their potential, and that they could cope with greater challenges – and relish them. So why do managers continue to act as though the same is not true of their staff? Is it only managers who are an under-utilised resource? Hardly likely. At a time when most organisations are looking for ways to increase efficiency and reduce costs we consistently fail to recognise one of the most cost-effective steps we can take: empowerment.

# Why Empower?

We have already looked at how empowerment can improve customer service. But it also offers other advantages to individuals and organisations. Personal benefits include the opportunity to enhance skills, which is important at a time when employment security is increasingly based less on initial qualifications and length of service than on the ability to acquire and market new skills and varied experience.

More and more organisations are moving towards the core/periphery model of staffing, in which a central permanent core of highly-skilled staff is supplemented on a flexible basis by contract, short-term and part-time staff as business demands dictate. Such a system will favour those who can demonstrate a wide range of skills, allowing them to respond flexibly to the needs of a series of employers. Staff who have only a narrow range of skills and experience will be at a marked disadvantage in the employment market-place.

Empowerment also offers staff a greater sense of achievement and, therefore, improved motivation. In an empowered workforce there is enhanced task significance: the sense that the job one does is important, not slight or trivial. Staff feel that they really can make a difference to important business outcomes, that what they do is vital (if only in a small way) to organisational success. Such a sense of having real impact can improve morale significantly. It may even help to reduce stress.

We tend to assume that stress is the prerogative of managers and is the result of having to make tough decisions under pressure, or juggle with complex ideas and issues. Yet research consistently shows that it is actually more stressful to be a humble factory operative than to be a managing director. Why? Because the managing director can exercise more control over his or her work. Lack of control over how one works is a significant factor in stress: the less control we can exercise the more stressed we are likely to become. Empowerment can increase people's sense of control by enabling them to make their own decisions about what they do and how they do it, to a much greater extent than under traditional management systems.

There are major organisational benefits too. One of the most important is increased organisational effectiveness. Empowerment achieves this by removing the blocks and brakes on performance which the tight control of more traditional approaches to management can produce. We all recognise the classic problems of bureaucracy, with its over-emphasis on regulation and authoritarian command. Yet such a management style can be a very efficient way to ensure conformity and consistency, and is an effective choice in stable situations, a slowly changing and predictable external environment, and where staff are of generally poor intellectual and educational calibre. However, it is a much less constructive way to manage people and organisations in a rapidly-changing world, where markets fluctuate or are hard to find and staff (whatever some ill-informed critics may say) are significantly better educated than their grandparents and great-grandparents were.

13

If organisations are to be able to react quickly and suitably to a fast-changing environment, they will need staff who are empowered to respond to circumstances as they find them without constantly having to seek advice or permission. This requires managers to place much greater trust in their staff's skill and knowledge and to remove many of the barriers which prevent them using these.

# Flexible management

This stress on speed of reaction may suggest the empowerment results in reactive management. Not so: it produces – and demands – flexible management. Reactive management, as its name implies, simply reacts to whatever may happen, without any clear plans or priorities. It is essentially backwards-focused and operates in a series of delays. Flexible management, however, empowers staff to take fast decisions based on a clear vision of success and explicit goals. It is essentially forward-focused, expects change and operates by trying to anticipate future demands as well as meet present ones.

Neither is empowerment a way for poor or lazy managers to evade their responsibilities or avoid discovery of their inadequacies. A truly empowered workforce needs, in fact, more highly-skilled and committed managers than more established forms of management such as bureaucracy or management by objectives. Such systems were developed largely to compensate for managerial and staff inadequacy rather than to harness skills. Empowerment requires the exercise of different management skills from those traditionally associated with older forms of management. These skills are also rather more complex and difficult to acquire, since they tend to be people-skills, requiring insight, imagination and maturity, rather than the more easily-taught skills which are essentially based on the rule book or the ledger. Empowerment makes more – not fewer – demands on managers. But it is also more rewarding.

To sum up: empowerment allows organisations to respond rapidly, flexibly and efficiently to customer and market demands. The result is reduced waste, delays and errors and a workforce in which staff are a fully-utilised resource. This is not mere benevolence. Staff represent a considerable investment. They are expensive to recruit and train. It makes good business sense to set up systems which produce the greatest return on that investment.

## 2

# Personal empowerment

Although this book is primarily about how to empower your staff and enable them to make a fuller contribution, the empowering manager first has to look at the extent to which he or she is empowered. How empowered are you? How do you know?

## Checking your restrictions

Most people feel that innumerable restrictions are placed around their sphere of action. Ambitious and competent managers, in particular, tend to sigh about these restrictions and chafe against constraints they feel hamper their freedom to act as they would wish in pursuit of management goals. But how realistic is this? The tendency is to assume that one lacks power and scope without ever really trying to find out just what the boundaries really are. Many people, no doubt, have less freedom to exercise initiative and discretion at work than they would like. But often we simply accept that restrictions exist, without actually checking that this is so.

So do you actually know – clearly – the boundaries of your own sphere of responsibility? Have you ever discussed these boundaries with your own line manager? Even if you have, have you ever tried to renegotiate them, to draw them more widely? If you don't know clearly what your boundaries of discretion are it's too easy to place tighter than necessary restrictions on your sphere of action. This can unduly restrict your capacity to manage effectively. You need to know how much freedom to act you have – or can take. This latter point is important. It is often possible to extend the boundaries of your sphere of action simply by acting as if you had the freedom to do so. As the old management adage says: it's often easier to seek forgiveness than ask permission. Simply assuming that you do have the freedom to act in a certain area may be the easiest way to establish that freedom as an accepted fact.

But freedom is not enough. Cynics might say that they have absolute freedom to do as they please – as long as they get it right! It's only when problems occur or mistakes are made that the boundaries are sharply drawn – rather more narrowly than before. This is, of course, a demoralising state of affairs, and one which, ultimately, tends to deter all but the bravest from exercising initiative. Few people will continue to take risks if they feel more likely to be punished for getting it wrong than to be praised for getting it right.

Unfortunately, many organisations are permeated with hostility to initiative and a punitive reaction to mistakes. Small wonder that staff at every level in such places seldom venture beyond the activities they know to be 'safe' and clearly within their remit. They choose to limit both their thought and action to a small percentage of what they might be. What a sad waste of human resources. Yet without a certain amount of sensible risk-taking, organisations seize up. They ossify into inflexible structures and systems which are too rigid to allow a speedy response to developing problems or opportunities. Such organisations run the real commercial risk that they will be unable to respond quickly enough to external or internal forces should the need arise. And that's a much more serious mistake than any individual is likely to make by simply trying to apply a little initiative and personal empowerment.

It is unlikely (though not, of course, actually impossible) that any single employee could make a sufficiently large error to close the company down. What is all too likely, however, is that a company which punishes risk-taking will fail to compete with more enlightened rivals and so lose its business to them. Now that's one mistake that *should* be punished! (And the market may do just that, eventually.)

If *you* find yourself working in an organisation where initiative is strongly discouraged, you need to take particular care not to perpetuate that attitude with your own staff. Successful empowerment depends, above all, on encouraging an enterprising approach to work and a non-punitive atmosphere. So even if you find yourself unduly restricted by hostility to initiative and heavy criticism it is important to build a different culture and climate within your own department or team. Your staff don't have to suffer in the same way you do. But this must start with yourself. You can't expect your staff to develop the confidence to use their own initiative if they don't see you exercising your own. In the jargon, you have to 'walk the talk' if you want your staff to be confident of their own ability to do so and convinced of the need.

17

Does this depend on your own manager? Not necessarily (though you could try lending him or her this book!). You can empower yourself so that you too no longer feel so restricted or nervous of stepping outside your present boundaries. Like any management task this is basically a matter of setting goals and making plans. But before we look at how you can start to set such goals and start making plans for your own empowerment, it's important to remember that even in relatively non-restrictive organisations the self-imposed barriers which managers place round their work tasks and responsibilities are frequently drawn much tighter – often by a wide margin – than those set by the organisation or line manager. People often have much more freedom to exercise discretion and act on initiative than they realise. What's more, this discretion may extend much further down the formal hierarchy of the organisation than one might think.

A new temp was coming to the end of her first week working as a receptionist in the Glasgow branch of an office equipment supply and maintenance company. There would normally have been five other staff in the office: two sales reps, two maintenance engineers and a man who rented desk space and secretarial support from the office equipment company. Unexpectedly, all five had been absent since she had started to work for the company. One of the engineers had a broken leg, the other was on holiday, and the two sales reps had just been sacked for embezzlement! Even the man who rented the office, who ran a small business supplying launderette equipment, was on holiday and had left instructions that he was not to be contacted except in a dire emergency.

On the Friday afternoon the telephone rang and an anxious voice explained that he needed a replacement part for a launderette machine very urgently indeed. The machine had completely broken down and the weekend – his busiest time – was fast approaching. When the temp explained that the manager concerned was away and could not be contacted the caller almost despaired. Without the spare part he would lose a substantial amount of business over the weekend. From his worried tone the temp suspected that such a loss would seriously threaten his business. She promised to see what she could do to help.

She asked the launderette owner to find out the part number of the component he needed and the name of the distributor. He didn't know the address or telephone number of the distributor but the temp guessed that they might have an office in or near London and so soon discovered their telephone number via directory enquiries. Then she called them. To her horror she was told that this part was no longer in production and therefore was not available.

Aware that the customer's business was at stake she decided to take a long shot and asked the supplier for the telephone number of the manufacturers, hoping that the necessary might be found lurking in the stores: it was worth a try, she thought.

She telephoned the manufacturers and was put through to the stores department: they didn't have one. But they did offer to put her through to the supervisor of the department which had manufactured the component. By this time it was mid-afternoon and the manufacturers were closing down for the weekend. Time was getting short. Once through to the supervisor, she explained the problem and asked if any of these components still remained anywhere in his department. They did not. Taking an even longer shot – especially at mid-afternoon on a Friday – she asked if there were any possibility of making the component as a one-off.

By this time the temp must have sounded nearly as desperate as the launderette owner. Perhaps that's why the supervisor – amazingly! – conceded that it might be possible to make the component: the equipment still existed and there were no major problems to prevent it. He agreed to make one there and then. But the problem still remained of how to get the component to Glasgow before the next day. She knew that the factory was somewhere in west London. There was just a chance it might be done. Pushing her luck still further she asked the supervisor if he could put the newly made component in a package and take it to Heathrow Airport to be put on the six o'clock flight to Glasgow. By this time the supervisor was caught up in the excitement of the problem, and agreed to do as she had asked.

So by four o'clock she was able to telephone a very grateful launderette owner with the news that he should meet the evening flight from Heathrow and he would be able to have his machine working by the next day. His business was able to operate without a hitch and the absent businessman retained a valuable customer he would otherwise have lost.

Now why did this temp take it upon herself to go to such lengths? Was she some high-powered and very experienced former PA used to dealing with such matters on behalf of her boss? No, she was a fifteen-year-old schoolgirl working during her school holidays. Then how was she able to exercise such initiative? Because she didn't know she couldn't! She had never worked in an office before so she simply didn't know that teenage temps aren't supposed to do such things. She just did what her own intelligence and common sense dictated she should: she hadn't been taught not to.

19

Too often we *are* taught not to exercise our initiative by bosses who punish any failure harshly and fail to applaud any initiative. That's no way to empower staff. Yet most people – like the teenage temp – are able to exercise far more common sense and initiative than we give them credit for. But if we don't make them feel safe when they take reasonable risks, if we criticise attempts at initiative and react with anger to well-meant errors, we stifle that initiative and demotivate people too.

So what happened to the girl in the story?

Well, the businessman came back from his holiday on the Monday and had enough sense to praise what she had achieved rather than tick her off for exceeding her powers or failing to contact him in what was, after all, an emergency. He was impressed by what she had done – and told her so. For her part, this was her first real job and she had been very nervous about whether she could do it. But she felt a real sense of achievement and proud that she had done a difficult job well. Her confidence in her own abilities grew.
Perhaps that's why she grew up to write a book about empowerment!

# Extending your boundaries

If a teenage temp can successfully extend the barriers around her sphere of action an experienced manager should certainly be able to do so. All it takes is a little thought and planning – and the courage to take the first step. Actually the first step is quite easy. A simple technique can help you to identify the changes you need to make.

Take a moment now to reflect on the boundaries you currently feel surround and restrict your freedom to act. Where are they now? How do you know?

First, divide a piece of paper as shown in Fig. 2.1, and in the first column list the boundaries you feel exist around what you are able to do. Try to consider your role at its widest. Think in terms of your staff management role as well as your production or service responsibilities. What action would you like to be able to take but feel unable to? What changes would you like to make but feel you can't? Write your list in the form 'I'd like to be able to . . .'. Try to make sure that what you want to do is in line with corporate, departmental and personal objectives: empowerment isn't about doing whatever one pleases. It's about a better way to reach the organisation's goals.

Now, in the middle column draw up a second list showing the evidence for the boundaries you identified in your first list. Think in terms of organisational and operational restrictions, such as lack of a proper budget of your own, or no access to the necessary information. Look for real evidence: your feeling that something is out of bounds is not enough. Don't include anything as evidence unless you know it to be true. Don't, for example, assume that you couldn't attend marketing department meetings from time to time unless you have actually asked to do so and been refused. Similarly, don't assume that your manager (or someone else) would object to something unless you have actually tried it and met an objection. Even if this has happened, do you *know* that it would happen again if your tried it now (and perhaps more

20

| I'd like to be able to . . . | Evidence | |
|---|---|---|
| | | |
| | | |
| | | |
| | | |
| | | |

**Fig. 2.1  Identifying your boundaries**

successfully)? If you can't think of any substantial evidence for any of your assumed boundaries, record that fact too.

Were there any areas where it was difficult to find real, hard evidence that you couldn't do as you wish? Was some of the evidence rather weak? Did you discover that you may be assuming that you can't do something without any clear evidence that this is so? So what's stopping you? You are – and no one else. You need to resolve now to take action in these areas. You can simply decide to empower yourself to take the action you would like to take or make the changes you want. How will you do that?

Well one thing you may need to do is change your own internal dialogue.

# Internal dialogue

Personal empowerment is not simply a matter of widening formal boundaries. To a large extent it depends on our internal dialogue: the kind of messages we send ourselves. We all talk to ourselves to some extent, even if we don't actually use words. But we tell ourselves what to expect in situations and from other people.

For example, confident people have an internal dialogue which tells them that they are competent, likeable people and that social events are likely to be pleasurable and interesting. People who lack self-confidence have an internal dialogue which tells them that they are dull or stupid and that, in social situations, everyone else will be much more attractive, witty or knowledgeable then they are.

But neither of these dialogues is necessarily based on any objective truth. We all know people whose lack of self-confidence seems at odds with their actual intelligence, attractiveness and charm. We may also know a few whose self-confidence seems equally ill-founded! Yet the people with the positive internal dialogue – whether realistic or not – cope better and probably achieve more than those whose negative internal dialogue unduly restricts them, causing them to be self-doubting and fearful. Our internal dialogue strongly affects how we see the world and how we behave in it. The problems of a negative internal dialogue are illustrated by the story of the farmer with the broken plough.

---

Farmer Jones had broken his plough. He was already late with his ploughing and didn't have time to wait while his plough was mended by the local blacksmith. The only solution he could think of was to borrow one from Farmer Brown, his neighbour, who had already ploughed his own fields. So he set off to walk up the valley to the neighbouring farm to borrow Farmer Brown's plough.

On the way he began to think of what Farmer Brown might say when he got there. His internal dialogue went something like this:

'Old Brown always seems to be ahead of me. He'll sneer at me because I'm so late with my ploughing. And he's sure to tell me off because I should have had my plough looked at by the blacksmith when I finished ploughing last year. That's what *he* always does. And he'll probably remind me that I still owe him a bag of seed corn from last year, when I ran out of my own. Trust him to have one to spare instead of running out, and to be so smug about it. He's always pointing out how much better organised his farm is. He even had a go at me about all those thistles in the bottom pasture last week. He really relishes it every time I have to borrow something from him. He just loves the chance to make me feel small. He's probably sitting up there now just waiting for his next chance to point out what a rotten farmer I am.'

By this time Farmer Jones had arrived at Farmer Brown's door. He knocked, rather loudly. As he waited for an answer his internal dialogue continued: 'If I ask to borrow his rotten plough he'll just use it as an excuse to brag about how much better he is than me. He's really going to enjoy me asking to borrow the plough. He'll probably gloat all the way to the Dog and Duck and tell everyone that I've messed up again. He's going to love every minute of that.'

Farmer Brown opened the door.

'You can keep your ruddy plough!' exploded Farmer Jones, and stalked off down the lane, leaving Farmer Brown looking very perplexed indeed.

---

Farmer Jones allowed his own internal dialogue to rob him of what he needed. How often do you do the same?

23

# Building a positive internal dialogue

Does your internal dialogue prevent your self-empowerment? How many of the fears you have about extending your boundaries or using your initiative at work are due to a negative internal dialogue which constantly stresses the potential pitfalls of what you might attempt and all the ways in which it might go wrong? If you haven't been able to identify any substantial evidence to support your view that you can't do what you'd like to do it may be that the real block to such progress is your own negative internal dialogue.

So how can you turn negative dialogue into positive dialogue? By focusing on the potential benefits of what you'd like to do. These benefits should include not just the benefits of the action itself, such as better use of staff resources or speedier response to customer enquiries, but how you will feel as a result. Make another list, this time with five columns, using the format shown in Fig. 2.2.

In the first column outline briefly the action you would like to

| Action | Fears | Probability | Prevent | Deal |
|--------|-------|-------------|---------|------|
|        |       |             |         |      |

**Fig. 2.2  Changing your internal dialogue from negative to positive**

take. In the second column, write down all the things you fear might happen if you take the action you planned. (Write the real nightmare scenario, up to and including being sacked!) In column three enter your subjective assessment of the probability of each fear actually happening, as a percentage. For example, if you realistically think that the odds that you'll be sacked are about one in ten, show this as 10%.

Now look at your list. How many of your fears seem likely to be a problem in reality? Far fewer than your internal dialogue has been telling you, I bet. But let's deal with those realistic fears. How could you prevent them happening? Use column four to plan some defensive action to prevent your worst and most pressing fears. With forethought, most problems of the kind you will have identified can be prevented. But suppose the worst does happen? How will you deal with it? Use the final column to plan your response. Could you mitigate its worst effects? Almost certainly. Could you even turn it to some advantage? Quite possibly.

Now look again at the positive outcomes. Are the benefits still worthwhile? Then what are you waiting for? You've planned to avoid disaster and even if the worst does happen you're prepared and you'll cope. At least you'll have tried. And, finally, remember that if you want to empower your staff you'll need to set an example by 'walking the talk' – and that means starting now! So, on a separate sheet of paper, make yourself a 'To do tomorrow' list (see Fig. 2.3). What steps can you take – tomorrow! – to move towards your goals. Remember, the only person putting a brake on your freedom to act in this area is you. Release the brake. Write down your list (with priorities identified) and resolve to take that first step towards empowerment for yourself and your staff tomorrow. If a teenage temp can do it, so can you.

| TO DO TOMORROW |
|---|
| 1 |
| 2 |
| 3 |

**Fig. 2.3   A 'To do tomorrow' list**

If you think it important to let people know what is going on (and in some cases it might be) send anyone who might be concerned a memo, letting them know what you are up to. It doesn't need to be a long justification of what you have decided, just a brief outline of what it is. But keep a copy of the memo. You may need to demonstrate at a later date that you did keep people informed. Be careful, too, of sending unnecessary memos: don't send one if the only result will be to panic someone into trying to stop you doing what you have planned (provided, of course, that you are sure that what you are doing is appropriate and in line with corporate goals). If you think that letting someone know what is going on is likely to produce resistance, you need to take the approach, described shortly for persuading others to give you the support or permission you need.

## Winning acceptance

Now look again at those boundaries (listed in Fig. 2.1) for whose existence you do have strong evidence. Who has the power to grant you permission to expand them? Write their names (or job titles) in the right-hand column of the sheet of paper, opposite the relevant action that you want to take (see Fig. 2.4).

| I'd like to be able to . . . | Evidence | Gatekeepers |
|------------------------------|----------|-------------|
|                              |          |             |

**Fig. 2.4   Identifying your boundaries: the gatekeepers**

Once you know who the gatekeepers (people who have the power to help or hinder you) are, the next step is to plan how to secure the support you need. The most effective way is to take a leaf out of the book of successful salespeople: sell benefit. In other words, try to identify the potential of what you are suggesting to provide some outcome that the gatekeeper will value, and then stress that persuasively. So, if you were able to do what you have identified, what would be the advantages to gatekeeper? Are these advantages likely to appeal to this particular person?

Not everyone is motivated by the same things. Some people are keen on making cost savings; others would prefer to be convinced that your proposal would solve a problem for them, or offer them a simpler life. Some would be keen to support an idea which increased their prestige or widened their personal empire. Others, again, would be motivated by ideas which improved the product or service you provide. People are motivated by a very wide variety of things. You need to identify the right levers to pull in each individual case.

Take another sheet of paper and divide it as shown in Fig. 2.5. Write the names of the gatekeepers in the left-hand column. Now write brief details of the change, etc., they control in the middle. On the right, jot down the potential benefits to each of them of what you propose. If you can think of more than one, so much the better.

Now you know what you need to do to achieve your aims: 'sell' each gatekeeper the benefits you have identified. This might best be done in a formal report setting out what you intend to do and

| Gatekeepers | Control | Benefits |
|---|---|---|
|  |  |  |

**Fig. 2.5   Selling the benefits**

the benefits this will provide. In some situations it might be better simply to discuss your ideas informally with the gatekeeper concerned. The best form of approach will vary from individual to individual, and from organisation to organisation. Just try to be sure that the approach you choose is the right one for you, the particular gatekeeper and the context.

Once you have the gatekeeper's agreement (and if you've identified some desirable benefits and 'sold' them well that should have happened) it might be a good idea to get the decision or permission you need in writing. This helps to avoid any possible problems in future, with the gatekeeper denying that permission was given. Even if this is unlikely, it can help to make you feel safer, knowing that you have 'proof' that your boundaries have been extended. If you have chosen a formal approach, such as a written report, try to get a written reply. Even if you choose to chat informally about your ideas you can create some kind of written record. Just send a memo to the gatekeeper concerned shortly after your conversation, outlining the discussion and the points you agreed. Keep a copy of the memo and of any written reply.

And that's it really. It's up to you now to make a start on the plans you had for all those areas you had thought were outside your remit. Look back at the boundaries you thought were encircling and restricting you. Do they seem different? How do you feel about this? Most people feel a sense of pleasurable challenge when they realise that they are actually far more free to make a real impact at work than they thought. There's a sense of release, a feeling that their skills and abilities will actually be put fully to use. That's the kind of feeling your staff could enjoy if you can empower them too. You've taken your first steps towards self-empowerment. It's time to turn your attention towards empowering others.

**3**

# Empowering others

Empowering others is essentially a matter of cultural change. It simply won't work unless the entire culture of the department (or, better still, organisation) changes substantially. Few existing cultures are able to support the types of change in attitude and practice that effective empowerment depends on. But in addition to cultural change, many organisations will need to achieve a change in their climate too. The wrong climate can blight the growth of empowerment before it's had a chance to blossom.

## Culture

Many people are confused about the meaning of the word 'culture' in management texts. Definitions abound, some of whose meaning is even more obscure than the word itself. The least complicated, most accessible and probably most useful definition of culture is that it is 'the way we do things round here'. This definition encompasses not just what is done in organisations, but the way in which it is done. And the way in which something is done relates closely to the collective attitudes and beliefs of the people who work in the organisation.

But despite the wide variety of beliefs, attitudes and practices in organisations, it is possible to identify some broad, general types of culture. In this book *Understanding Organisations*, Charles Handy identifies these cultural types as those based on power, role, task and person.

## POWER CULTURE

Power culture is probably the earliest and most traditional form of culture found in organisations. It is typically found in organisations where a charismatic entrepreneur has developed the organisation by sheer personal energy. It exists not only in commercial ventures but just as commonly in charities and voluntary organisations. In such a culture there tends to be one central power source, usually the entrepreneur, from which all directives flow and where all the important strings are pulled together and held. Because organisational ideas tend to be the product of one mind (or a very small group of minds) and because such organisations are small, they are able to change direction easily and respond quickly to developing opportunities. Formal systems tend to be few, however, and communication tends to radiate out, like the spokes on a bicycle wheel, from the power hub at the centre.

In such organisations, power is heavily vested in the centre, from which a web of control spreads out. It therefore severely restricts the opportunity for anyone who is not close to the centre to have any impact on direction or how things are done. They are also very dependent on the central power source. If that source dies or departs, the organisation can find itself in deep trouble. The loss can leave a power vacuum in which people vie with one another to take over the central position, sometimes resulting in bitter fights. Whilst this is going on the organisation lacks direction and may drift badly.

Also, though such a culture is able to respond quickly to new opportunities or threats, and is an effective one for small, new organisations, it can easily become a victim of its own success. It tends to hit trouble once a certain stage of growth has been achieved. After a certain size a heavily-centralised culture can lose touch with customers (because the power source is no longer able to stay close to them) and can find itself having increasing difficulty simply running the new, larger organisation since formal systems are few and communication has tended to be informal rather than planned and controlled. Individuals within the organisation who may have thrived in the slightly piratical style of culture may have great difficulty adapting to the need for more formal and systematic management. At this stage such organisations typically 'die', either by collapse or take-over. They can be heady, exciting places to work for those at or near the centre, but they seldom make much use of the talents, skills and knowledge of the rest of the workforce, including less senior managers. They can also seem tough or downright hostile places in which to work, and though they may be tolerant of the means by which results are achieved, they are seldom tolerant of errors. Such organisations offer little power to anyone but those at the hub. That's one reason, perhaps, that they typically fail to survive in this form for very long.

A rare exception to this rule seems to be the Virgin empire headed by Richard Branson. Here, it would seem, is a typically entrepreneurial, charismatic founder who developed a multi-million-pound business from a standing start to the point where it is able to see off such long-established rivals as British Airways. Yet this picture would be misleading. Richard Branson has achieved this feat by deliberately not allowing any individual business venture to grow beyond a certain size. Once any of his companies has grown large enough to stand on its own feet he hives it off as a separate venture, complete with its own largely autonomous management team. In this way he empowers not individuals but companies and their managers, who are charged simply with getting on with the job of running the company as they see fit provided they meet some broad corporate goals and objectives. As a corporate strategy it seems highly successful, offering both growth and flexibility. What is less clear is whether even these smaller organisational units are able to make full use of the potential of those individuals who are not close to the power at the centre.

## ROLE CULTURE

If an organisation is able to sustain growth beyond the stage which can be supported by a power culture it will typically need to adopt a new culture, one based on roles. This is the type of culture most often associated with large, bureaucratic structures with a strongly hierarchical, pyramidical management structure and many formal systems and procedures. Within such cultures power stems from occupying a particular role or position. Though much mocked it is actually a very effective way to manage large organisations with clear and unchanging goals in a stable environment.

And that's exactly the problem. Few organisations these days operate in such a stable sphere. Even public sector organisations – the type most often associated with bureaucratic power cultures – no longer exist in a stable environment. They too need to be much lighter on their feet and more flexible in response to a changing world. But many organisations still exist in this form and can find themselves in difficulties if, as such cultures typically do, they fail to spot important commercial straws in the wind. They tend to disregard what other smaller companies are doing, assuming that massive size and commercial power protect them from the scramblings after business of their more modest competitors. And where they do find themselves in difficulty they tend to try to use sheer commercial force to defeat the opposition.

One classic example of this is IBM, which failed to spot the microcomputer revolution until it had lost its opportunity to dominate the market. IBM was powerful enough to impose a hardware standard but failed to capitalise on it with software. Later attempts to catch up were largely unsuccessful since they were based less on a clear appreciation of customer needs than on an attempt to use corporate muscle to impose IBM's own standard on the market. Smaller, newer companies with a more entrepreneurial, power-based culture, such as Bill Gates' Microsoft, were much closer to the customer and able to supply what was needed faster and more effectively. It's interesting to note, though, that as Microsoft itself has grown, it, too, seems to be adopting something of the cultural style of its Big Blue rival.

This distance of corporate decision-making from the customer is a result of the long chains of command typically found in hierarchical role-based cultures. Worse, such organisations commonly have few, if any, means of tapping the knowledge held by staff further down the power chain who are closer to the commercial realities of the context in which it operates. Recognising these problems, many such organisations have recently attempted to flatten the hierarchy by removing one or more layers of management. But whilst this may help, it cannot, by itself, achieve the kind of fully utilised workforce that empowerment offers. Flattened organisation structures go some way towards avoiding the worst problems of role cultures, but unless the culture itself changes many difficulties will remain.

The problem for an individual manager in such an organisation is that a single person – even one at or close to the top of the pyramid – is seldom able to exert much influence on the overall culture of such an organisation, let alone its actual structure.

33

## TASK CULTURE

A less common type of culture is that based on the task itself. It is most commonly found where the organisational structure takes a matrix or net form in which horizontal lines of communication are as important as vertical ones. Such structures are typically, found in newer, small, technology-based organisations or in consultancies of various kinds where much of the work is carried out in project teams. In such structures, although there may also be formal managerial and administrative roles, these tend to be superimposed on the basic form of the project team. Such teams may have a limited, and perhaps quite short, lifespan and may re-form with a different composition when one project is finished and another about to begin. The teams usually operate with a fair degree of autonomy within their project parameters. This culture and structure offer a considerable degree of job satisfaction to staff and are an effective way to organise work in situations where staff have a high degree of expertise.

But it is certainly no panacea. It only works well if teams don't have to compete for work or scarce resources, and in contexts where the goals are clear. It also relies heavily on the motivation of the teams themselves since formal management control is all but impossible. Nor is it necessarily a guarantee that the teams will be close to the customers and their needs. In fact, a process called 'group-think', in which team cohesion and mutual support begin to take precedence over realistic appraisal of external events and problems, can seriously hamper such teams' ability to respond to outside threats or opportunities. This type of structure is seldom the predominant form in any organisation other than the very smallest because it is so difficult to control. Problems may also occur, as we have seen, if teams become isolated and detached from both customers and organisational objectives.

34 Where matrix structures and cultures do exist they are commonly superimposed on a classic pyramidal structure and within an overall role-based culture. In some larger companies whose business relies on the deployment of technical specialists these two cultures and systems sometimes operate side by side, each with its own promotion and reward system. Some of the larger oil and petrochemical companies, for example, have separate pay and promotion scales for their technical and administrative/ managerial staff. Their management and administration structures are based on role culture and a pyramidal structure, whilst their technical staff operate largely in a task-based culture and team structure.

It's by no means a perfect system. Technical staff tend to feel that the management skills they actually use are unrecognised and undervalued by the system. But what it does do is formalise the *de facto* situation which operates in a great many organisations today, where there is increasing use of team-working, work cells and the like.

## PERSON CULTURE

Finally, some organisations operate within a person culture in which there are few management structures, and where these do exist their purpose is to support the activities of the individuals rather than control them. It is a less common form than any of the previous three and is usually associated with loose groups of individuals with a high degree of expertise who have come together to share opportunities and resources.

It is found in such places as barristers' chambers and was the original form taken by academic institutions. (Its structure is sometimes referred to as collegiate.) It permits a high degree of autonomy to the individuals within it, who are given the widest possible opportunity to exercise and develop their skills. At the level of the individuals themselves it is highly responsive to external demands and opportunities, but it cannot easily harness those individuals into a joint effort even if a situation demands it.

Its potential for adoption in most larger organisations is obviously limited, yet it is probably the kind of culture that most people would feel most comfortable within.

35

# Empowerment culture

As we have seen, there are number of different types of culture and organisational structure. These raise a number of questions in relation to empowerment. Is it actually possible to empower staff (or even oneself) fully within any of these existing cultures and structures? Or is some completely new structure and culture required? Can one really implement empowerment within just one part of an organisation whilst the rest continues to exist in an inimical form?

## STRUCTURES AND EMPOWERMENT

The most common form of all structures is the hierarchical pyramid. It exists in some form, however vestigial, in virtually all organisations which consist of more than a very few people. As soon as anyone appoints an assistant of any kind, a hierarchy is formed. This is true even of power-cultures and task cultures. Even these usually appoint someone to type the letters or answer the telephones.

In fact the idea of a hierarchy is inherent in the very essence of management. We rarely consider anyone a 'proper' manager unless they have some line management responsibility for at least one (and usually more than one) person. The more people someone has within their span of control the more likely we are to regard them as having substantial management responsibilities. Even project teams operating within a pure matrix structure usually have a formal leader, and that leader is normally a senior member of the organisation.

So it is hardly surprising that most people think of the task of management as being to preside over a pyramid (however small) of other staff, planning, directing and controlling their activity. Modern management theory may have caused the chain of command to shorten as companies de-layer their hierarchies and flatten their pyramids, but they still exist in some form almost everywhere. We have already seen how this structure can make rapid response to customer needs or external demands difficult. Even in its flattened form senior managers are typically at least four steps away from the external customer. So how can a manager operating within a hierarchical, pyramidal structure empower staff and bring about the necessary cultural changes to support that initiative?

As a manager within an organisation you probably have few, if any, opportunities to make radical alterations to the structure of the organisation. You are likely to have only limited opportunities to instigate matrix or collegiate structures. You are still less likely to be able to exert much influence on the overall culture of the organisation as a whole. But what you can do is to change the way you manage within a pyramidal structure. You can invert your own particular pyramid so that you play a supporting, rather than a figurehead, role. And you can try to develop a culture which supports empowerment within your own particular sphere of influence and a climate which fosters its growth.

## THE INVERTED PYRAMID

Managers can look at their own management pyramid in two ways: from above, looking down the layers of the hierarchy, and inverted. Viewed from above the manager's role seems to be primarily that of leadership and command; viewed inverted, it looks very different indeed. From this perspective the manager's primary responsibilities are now revealed to be offering a firm, stable foundation for the department or team, and providing reliable support and maintenance. This is a quite different way to look at the role of a manager and it requires the exercise of a different – and in many ways more challenging – set of skills from those associated with management from above. We look at those skills in the next chapter.

37

We are so accustomed to looking at the pyramid in one particular way, in which we regard managers as being 'above' their staff (who even describe themselves as working 'underneath' or 'below' their boss) that the full implications of inverting the pyramid can take some time to sink in. Yet there is no particular reason for us always to see it that way. Inverting it does not change the pattern of span of control or lines of command in any way. What it does do is expose to scrutiny the assumptions on which so much of management has been based in the past. For there is no reason at all to assume that a manager is, or ought to be, in a position 'over' that of the staff. Such terminology undervalues not just the staff concerned but their skills, competence and intelligence too. Inverting the pyramid focuses attention on the staff, starting with those who have usually been regarded as the 'lowest', and who are also those closest to the customer. The inverted pyramid places these front-line staff where they belong: on top of any good manager's set of priorities. In the inverted pyramid managers – and supervisors – provide staff with the support they need to perform what is, after all, the primary task of any organisation or department: meeting customer needs.

In empowerment culture power is conducted to where it will have most effect: the interface between the organisation (or department) and those on whose custom it relies. The role of the manager is primarily to maximise the effective and efficient delivery of customer service by providing the necessary resources, guidance, etc. so that this can happen. The role of the front-line staff themselves is not merely to deliver that service but to ensure that the right kind of information about customers' needs filters back through the organisation to the manager, who can then use this to co-ordinate future action and developments throughout the pyramid.

The empowering manager, as we have seen, needs to be *an* authority, rather than *in* authority, supporting an inverted pyramid, in which power and responsibility are shared and the flow of information is multi-directional.

38

## Creating a climate of empowerment

Looking at issues of culture and structure in organisations reveals some of the difficulties managers may face as they try to empower staff, as well as one important way to look afresh at the organisation pyramid so that opportunities for empowerment can be seen.

There is one aspect of organisational life, however, where every manager really does have substantial opportunity to bring about significant and worthwhile change: climate. The term 'climate' refers, quite simply, to what it feels like to work in a particular organisation, department or team. Climates are typically described as 'warm' or 'cold', but other, less weather-related terms are important too. Organisational climate can also be described as feeling hostile, or confusing, or supportive to those who work there.

How does your organisation feel to you? Does it feel safe, or scary, to work there? Do you feel confident or confused about corporate objectives? These are questions which we don't always ask our-selves as often as we should. Recognising how the organisation feels to us as managers is important. It may give some inkling as to how it feels to staff. But the same organisation can feel very different to different individuals and to groups of staff at different levels.

In my work with managers from a wide range of organisations and levels within them I typically find that perception of climate varies enormously depending on a particular manager's position in the organisation's hierarchy. Senior managers are much more likely to describe their organisation as supportive, enabling, facil-itative, people-centred, flexible, and the like. Middle or junior managers, on the other hand, are more likely to experience their organisations as hostile, restrictive, petty in the application of rules, rigid and punitive. Sometimes the two are actually talking about the same place of work.

39

So it's very important to try to find out how the organisation or department actually feels to your staff. Don't just assume they feel what you feel, or that you already know what they feel. *Ask* them.

Now that's not as simple as it might seem. Staff may be reluctant to admit to you, their manager, that they are less than perfectly happy. In fact, if your staff consistently tell you that everything is fine, warning bells should start ringing. They may be nervous of voicing complaints in case you think they are being difficult. Or they may simply feel under peer pressure to present a united front that all is well. Paradoxically, one of the problems of the current emphasis on teamwork is that healthy dissent can be suppressed by members of the team if they feel that any kind of critique might be regarded as letting the side down. This is not a very healthy or productive state of affairs. It's probably a much healthier sign if your staff *do* have some criticisms to make. This at least suggests that they are being honest with you, and with their fellow team members.

So you need to give some careful thought to how you are going to seek information about the current climate. One obvious choice, the anonymous questionnaire, can be an effective approach in some contexts. If you decide to use this method try to keep it as brief and informal as possible – there is no need to use a sledgehammer to crack this particular nut. You're just trying to find out how much the current climate is likely to support your plans for empowerment, or whether it needs to be changed first. However, even a simple questionnaire may be too formal a method for some organisational contexts or staff teams. If yours is such an organisation or team then a face-to-face interview might work better. But how can you be sure that staff really feel able to express themselves honestly? If they don't, they're hardly likely to tell you that either! (And they may even say the opposite.) One way round that is to ask a third party – someone you trust and to whom your staff will feel safe to express their views – to interview people for you. This will probably work better if you choose someone other than your own manager. A skilled outside consultant is probably best of all if your budget will stretch to it. If you are planning empowerment on a large scale you may need the additional support and advice of a consultant to help you plan and implement the rest of the project too.

Whichever approach you choose, remember that the aim of the exercise is to get some sense of how the present climate seems to your staff, even if this is very different from how it seems to you. You may discover some surprises. Remember too that you are doing this to find out whether you need to take steps to create a climate of greater trust and openness in order to support your moves towards empowering your department or team. It's worth spending some time and effort to get this right.

In trying to discover what kind of climate your organisation or department seems to have to your staff you need to focus on two key factors. These are trust and openness.

## TRUST

Of all the factors affecting empowerment this is, perhaps, the most important, a point this book will stress throughout. Trust between you and your staff is a prerequisite of successful empowerment. And nowhere is trust a more significant issue than in your capacity to tolerate errors. You must be able to accept that errors will occur from time to time, even without empowerment, and you must be able to tolerate well-intentioned errors made in the pursuit of appropriate goals. This requires you to trust your staff to use their initiative and make their own judgements, even if these judgements are not always identical to those you would have made in the same circumstances. Your staff need to feel that you can trust them to take sensible risks if necessary in pursuit of clear and agreed goals. And they must be able to trust you to tolerate the occasional errors they may make in doing so.

Tolerance of errors does not, of course, mean turning a blind eye to incompetence, or to stupid, pointless mistakes. What it does mean is that any manager who seriously wishes to empower staff must foster a climate of mutual trust in which people feel safe to go beyond their immediate remit if they see good reason to do so, even at the risk of a mistake.

41

Now this will obviously result in errors of some sort being made from time to time. That's bound to happen. When it does, the wise manager will take at least as much account of the praiseworthy reasons for making the error as of the error itself. The golden rule is this: staff need to feel that they are more likely to be criticised for not trying than for not succeeding.

Of course repetition of avoidable mistakes should never be acceptable. But this is what is most likely to happen where managers criticise the error but don't explain how it could have been avoided, or how it might be put right. This kind of response leaves staff with nowhere to go but into the kind of hurt and sullen resentment which practically guarantees that they'll never try to exercise their initiative again. So if people do get it wrong, it's essential to tell them how to put it right, or how to avoid the same thing happening again.

And must it be said that shows of temper have no place in a

working environment? Sadly it must, since too many managers seem to feel that the only way to prevent a mistake being repeated is to yell and bawl or – worse – hiss their criticisms furiously at the hapless miscreant. That's no way to treat a grown adult. It's certainly no way to treat someone you want to empower. You, as manager, have both the right and the duty to make sure that staff understand that a mistake has been made. You do *not* have the right, much less the duty, to try to make them feel small or incompetent about it.

Do your staff feel they can admit to making a mistake? This is not simply a moral point. It's a practical one. If staff come to fear your reaction to errors and mistakes they are unlikely to risk making any. That means they will place unnecessary restrictions around what they are prepared to risk doing, even if they can see the need. Remember the rule that staff need to feel that they are more likely to be criticised for not trying than for not succeeding? Perhaps it needs an addition: staff should never have to fear trying to do something right, even if they get it wrong.

There's another point: if staff fear your angry response to any errors or mistakes, they are much more likely to try to cover them up than admit to them, and that's the last thing you need. You need to be able to trust your staff, and they need to be able to trust you. If you are to provide your customers, internal or external, with the products and services they need, then you cannot afford to risk a climate in which errors and mistakes are hidden away or denied out of fear.

This brings us to the other key point: openness.

## OPENNESS

If staff feel they can be open with you, even about their mistakes, you will have taken a large stride towards an empowering climate. If they can also express doubts and even criticism freely, then you are a step nearer still. It's important that they should be

able to trust you, and that they should feel that yᴗ
their appraisal of you.

In a truly empowered organisation or department appraisa.
whether formal or informal – will always be a two-way process.
This is because you need to know whether you are meeting your
staff's expectations of you every bit as much as they need the same
feedback from you. If your role as an empowering manager is to
provide the kind of guidance and support your staff need to perform their roles to the best of their ability, then you will need to
hear from them whether they think you are achieving this. You
will need to give some thought to how this might be achieved.
Finding out their views on the climate of organisation or department is only the first step in that process.

The other side of openness, of course, is the extent to which staff
feel that you are open with them. Do they feel that you keep them
fully informed not just about what's happening but about your
thoughts and plans too? Do you seem an open book or a dark
horse? Staff need to have access to your thoughts and ideas if they
are to feel able to trust you. If they feel you have too great a
tendency to keep your thoughts hidden they may begin to worry
about what these might be. That's not conducive to a climate of
openness. Your staff need to be kept informed as fully as possible.
That way you will be able to develop a climate and atmosphere in
which you can *all* share thoughts and ideas freely.

# 4

# Leading from behind

In chapter 3 I discussed inverting the traditional pyramidal management structure to be found in most organisations so that the front-line staff – those nearest the customer – were at the top of the inverted pyramid, supported rather than controlled by supervisors and managers. Such a reversal of the normal way of looking at organisations clearly has implications too for the way in which they should be managed. Such a non-traditional view of organisations requires the application of some non-traditional management skills. But let's look first at those traditional skills. Are they all redundant in empowered organisations?

## Traditional management skills

From Henri Fayol in the nineteenth century to the present day, management theorists have attempted to list the skills and tasks of successful management. The lists vary, of course, but few would dispute that the following skills and tasks are essential to the traditional role of the manager:

- planning
- communicating
- co-ordinating
- motivating
- controlling
- directing
- leading.

But is this list still appropriate to an empowered organisation and an empowering manager?

There can be little argument about such skills as planning, communicating, co-ordinating, and motivating. The manager who lacks these skills will not be able to implement any empowerment programme successfully. Indeed all four are essential if empowerment is to be truly effective.

The introduction of empowerment requires careful planning if it is to be accepted by staff as a new and better way of working. The detailed planning of an empowerment programme is discussed in a later chapter. But planning is not only important during the initial phase in which you introduce this way of working to your staff: it is essential on a continuing basis. Staff cannot exercise initiative and develop their own ideas if they have no idea of the direction in which they should be moving. Clear plans and goals are a prerequisite of effective empowerment. Without the clear sense of direction which proper planning provides staff lack the guidelines they need to support their endeavours. Obviously, too, plans which are not communicated clearly, in the right way and at the right time, are no use whatever.

45

Co-ordination, too, is vital. Empowerment can too easily degenerate into everyone acting individualistically as the whim takes them, rather than independently but in a co-ordinated way. Effective co-ordination, of course, relies on clear plans, properly communicated. If effort is to be collective, rather than just a disconnected mish-mash, it is essential that the manager co-ordinate the work of the organisation or department with skill and determination.

And the need for motivation need hardly be stressed. Fortunately, handled well, empowerment is a potent motivational system in itself. However, as a later chapter explains, staff do not always greet empowerment with the automatic enthusiasm which some of its proponents might lead you to expect. On the contrary, you may actually encounter considerable resistance to the idea at first. The 'old' management skill of motivating staff by convincing them of the real benefits to be gained will certainly be necessary if you are to gain not just acceptance of the idea but the wholehearted commitment to it on which its ultimate success will depend.

But what about those other 'old' skills: controlling, directing and leading. Are they anachronistic in modern management contexts? It's largely a question of emphasis. Even in an empowered organisation there may still be occasions when a manager has to exert control: over budgets, for example. And, paradoxically, it may require all of a manager's skills in directing and leading to set the empowerment process in train in order to overcome staff resistance to the idea at first. So, far from being redundant skills, they remain as important as ever. What needs to change is the frequency and emphasis with which they are deployed as the empowerment process becomes established.

46

If you retain a management style which is, overall, largely directive and controlling you will never achieve empowerment in your staff. They will continue to regard the success of the organisation or department as primarily *your* responsibility, not theirs. They will continue to expect you to make all the major decisions and take all the risks. You may also risk perpetuating a climate in which staff prefer not to exercise initiative in case it doesn't meet with your approval.

Of course there will always be occasions and situations in which someone has to take charge and give a clear lead. There's clearly no point in calling a staff meeting to thrash out collectively the pros and cons of the order in which the building should be evacuated in the event of a fire if it's actually burning at the time! At a time like that the essential thing is that someone should give clear directions and exercise firm control over their execution – and no arguing. (But would that person have to be you, I wonder?)

In general, however, the sort of situation which requires that kind of highly directive and controlling management style are few and far between in a well-run organisation or department. That kind of approach is necessary and, in the long term, productive only in situations such as short-term crises or emergencies. Few well-organised organisations or departments have such short time-horizons on a regular basis. (If yours does this is a problem you may need to address. Is what you do really crisis management? Or is it management *by* crisis?). In general, the longer the time-scale over which the proposed action will be carried out the more it is essential to avoid such an essentially authoritarian management style.

It's not the case, then, that these 'old' skills are redundant in an empowered organisation, merely that a change in emphasis is required. But are these 'old' skills enough in a new approach such as empowerment? Doesn't a new management approach like this require new management skills too? It certainly does.

# New management skills

Empowerment, far from being an easy ride for a lazy or uncommitted manager, makes considerable additional demands on managerial skills and resources. It also requires the deployment of a new set of skills. The new managerial skills required in an empowered organisation include:

- enabling
- facilitating
- consulting
- collaborating
- mentoring
- supporting.

## ENABLING

Enabling means ensuring that your staff have all resources they need to be fully empowered. These may include sufficient time, personnel, money, etc. to achieve agreed goals. But it goes beyond the provision of such tangible or measurable resources. Enabling is also about how your staff feel about their own competence. The

47

enabling manager tries to ensure that staff also have the necessary self-confidence to cope with aplomb with the new demands that empowerment places on them, as well as with the opportunities it offers. This means not only offering encouragement and advice, but also making sure that staff have the full range of skills and knowledge they need to be effective members of the team.

Training has for too long been regarded as A Good Thing – if we could afford it. It has been treated as something which can be reduced or even cut altogether when budgets are under pressure: a perk rather than the raw material on which the organisation depends. Yet it really is just as much a raw material as any other that the organisation uses. Without it the 'real' raw materials (and that includes information or services too) which your organisation provides will never reach the necessary standard to compete successfully against your more perspicacious competitors. Research shows what enlightened organisations and shrewd managers have always known: that companies which invest significantly in training have a better survival and growth record than those which don't.

If you truly wish to enable your staff to reach your goals you need to make sure that they have not only the physical and financial resources they need but the personal ones too. And that means being prepared to invest properly in training. No one expects people to produce good work with poor physical tools. Whatever the old saying about bad workers blaming their tools may suggest, we recognise that poor equipment produces poor products. So it is essential to ensure that your staff are well equipped with the best possible intangible tools – knowledge, skill, understanding, experience – and that needs properly-planned, systematic training for all.

## FACILITATING

The skill of facilitation is perhaps the most fundamental of those needed by an empowering manager. The empowering manager regards it as a central management task to remove all the blocks, hurdles and delays which prevent staff from doing the very best work of which they are capable. Some of these blocks consist of inadequate information, skill or knowledge. Training has an important role to play here, too. But often these problems are due to organisational rules and procedures which actually hinder, rather than help, peak performance. Blocks – (rules which exist to prevent something happening) and hurdles (systems and procedures which staff have to negotiate their way through) have usually been put in place in order to assist management control. They exist to *prevent* certain things happening – mistakes, errors, etc. – rather than to aid progress. But companies with successful experience of Total Quality Management know the truth of the adage that you can't screen errors out, you have to build Quality in. The more error-trapping you do, the more people come to rely on the error-trappers to weed out their mistakes and botch-ups. Making people individually and collectively responsible for their *own* Quality not only helps to reduce costly errors but frees up processes enormously too.

49

Both blocks and hurdles are a prime cause of delays for staff and customers. Think about that procedure which was still common at many supermarkets and shop tills a few years ago: calling a supervisor every time a customer wanted to pay by cheque. Why? I always wanted to ask. Are supervisors more gifted than their till-operator colleagues at detecting fraud by looking at a customer's signature? Is this a gift that they mysteriously receive when they don the sacred mantle (a slightly posher overall) of authority? Hardly likely. This was a classic example of a block. It was a practice with its roots firmly entrenched in lack of trust and lack of training. It didn't happen in every supermarket or every chain-store. Were those which didn't think they needed this procedure losing oodles of cash on bent cheques? Of course not. How do I know? Because in recent years fewer and fewer shops put their customers through this irritating and time-consuming procedure. They now trust their staff to exercise a little common sense and good judgement, and train them to make sure they can do this properly.

But many of organisations have similar practices designed to weed out errors. Are they all necessary? Almost certainly not. The empowering manager will recognise that whilst some such controls may still be necessary, the majority are probably not. Facilitation means looking at what your staff need to do, then providing as smooth a path through that as you possibly can. Look at the systems and procedures which your staff currently operate. Are they all really essential? How many would no longer be necessary if you were to trust your staff, and train them properly? And how many of those are actually getting in the way of their ability to serve your customers?

Talk to your staff. Ask them which systems restrict their freedom to respond to customer needs, and which slow them down. Watch them at work. Can you see any practices which need to be looked at again? Administrative procedures are typically those most likely to include over-checking, poor work planning and delays. Administrative procedures which are partly – but only partly – computerised are often worst of all. Look for both blocks (designed to stop something happening) and hurdles (systems and procedures which restrict what staff are allowed to do). Look out also for delays of any kind, especially if you can't immediately see why they occur. Such delays are often a symptom of unnecessary rules and procedures.

Again, you may find the services of outside consultants useful here because they can see systems and procedures with a fresh eye, undimmed by familiarity. They can also ask the apparently naive or downright silly question about why a procedure is followed, which those closest to a situation might not think to ask. Apparently daft questions often produce some very useful answers, I have found. A consultant is also more able to spot when a system has been designed around a problem (or problem person) instead of trying to solve the problem (or deal with the person) directly: a very common situation and one which can act as a powerful brake on organisational effectiveness at every level.

So the empowering manager will do everything possible to ensure that obstacles facing staff are removed or reduced, so that staff can give their best efforts unhindered by unnecessary blocks, hurdles and delays.

## CONSULTING

The importance of recognising the knowledge and experience possessed by those staff nearest to the customers has already been stressed. Clearly, then, the empowering manager will wish to harness this knowledge and experience and make good use of it. This means consulting staff not just about day-to-day matters (though this is important) but about strategic issues too.

This needs to go beyond merely asking for opinions or ideas. Certainly, the good old-fashioned suggestions box still has a part to play (though do make sure you make active use of it). I worked as a consultant to one organisation where, I was told, they had once had a suggestions scheme which, after a successful start, eventually fell into abeyance. Time passed and most of the boxes were recycled for other purposes or simply disappeared. The managing director told me that one day, as he was practising his skills of management-by-walking-about, he spotted an old forgotten suggestions box on a wall in a dark corner. The box was fixed very firmly indeed to the wall (which is perhaps why it was still there) and its lid had become stuck shut.

51

The MD, realising that this sent a rather demoralising message to staff, insisted that the box be removed and opened immediately. He resolved to take immediate action on any reasonable suggestions it contained and to ensure that the whole company were told about these. He therefore watched for the best part of half an hour while two strong men struggled to chisel the box from the wall before carrying it to his office where they jemmied the lid open. Pleased, he peered inside. The box was completely empty. The lesson? Suggestions schemes only work if they are actively managed and not allowed to sink into disuse. A good suggestions scheme needs to become a central part of the organisation's culture ('the way we do things here'). Indeed, unless you have some way in which you regularly and systematically try to find out what front-line staff think needs to be done you'll never succeed in meeting your customers' requirements. Yet few organisations have such a system.

When I feel that I have received poor service due to a system or procedural problem (rather than just plain poor service) I always make point of asking whether the person I'm dealing with has some way of feeding my complaint back through the system to someone who has the power to change it. I almost always receive one of two replies: 'No' or 'You'll have to contact customer services.' Neither of these is satisfactory.

In the first case, if no procedure exists then not only do I, the customer, feel undervalued but the hapless worker does too. If you don't have a system to harvest customer complaints at the point where they first reach the organisation then you send a clear message to those front-line troops that their knowledge of customer requirements is too trivial to warrant the serious attention of an important manager. You also send a message to your customers that they don't really matter to you either. This can make them rather irate. And guess who has to deal with that? That's right, the one group of people who may know how the problem might be avoided. Any system which leaves staff at the front line without a means of communicating problems back to you, the manager, cannot possibly be said to be empowering.

Often such problems seem trivial to a busy manager, but are only too noticeable to both customers and staff. For example, a well-known supermarket chain marks its cut-price offers by sticking a little, yellow, handwritten price tag over the barcode. The stickers are brightly coloured so that they are easily seen by both customers and checkout staff. They have to be peeled off before the goods can be passed over the optical reader. This is, of course, a very efficient way to make sure that the checkout operator doesn't overcharge the customer by just using the normal barcode reader. It must have seemed like a very good idea in the office of whichever manager thought of it. Unfortunately, the little yellow stickers don't come off easily or in one piece, but only with great difficulty and in several tiny, fiddly bits (possibly to stop dishonest customers moving the stickers to other products). This may not be much of a problem if only one such item is in your shopping trolley. However, if like me, you're a real bargain hunter it becomes intensely irritating to watch, as the minutes to your next appointment tick by, while the checkout operator fiddles around with the little yellow labels on item after item. It's also very annoying for all the people in the queue behind who also get held up unnecessarily.

One day I asked my usual questions. Do all the checkout operators find it a problem? Yes, they certainly do. Have any of the managers ever asked you about it? No. Is there any system – such as a suggestions box, perhaps – which would allow you to tell managers that customers are being held up whilst you fiddle like this? No, nothing of the kind. And lest any manager from this supermarket chain should want to dispute this on the ground, perhaps, that such a scheme does exist, the point is that the checkout operator did not know about it. And what staff don't know about they can't use.

Sometimes, of course, I get the other answer: contact customer services. Now I have a deep-seated aversion to giving free consultancy advice (a view my bank manager supports heartily). So I never do contact their customer services department. But how many other people do either? Certainly, if there were a major problem with a product or a service then I might. But the issues I am describing here are the sort of minor irritations which don't seem worth making a huge fuss about, but which nonetheless reflect badly on the organisation and its staff. Too small to make a formal complaint about (given all the time and energy that would require), they may, however, be large enough to make me take my custom elsewhere in future.

Is that what customer service departments are for? To pass on customers to competitors? Of course, there's nothing wrong with having a special department with staff who are skilled at dealing with complaints – but it's not enough. If that's all there is, such a department may be counter-productive. What's more, it's no substitute for empowering front-line staff to deal directly with minor irritations and complaints themselves. Nor is it a sufficient means of picking up customer complaints. Even where a customer services department exists it is still vital to have a parallel system for harvesting ideas and issues which need resolving from front-line staff. That's why direct, active, regular consultation of these staff is so important. Of course, such consultation needn't always be face to face. An *active* suggestions box scheme can work perfectly well, providing that staff have faith that their ideas will be taken seriously. But a suggestions scheme only allows people to offer solutions to problems, not simply to notify you of the existence of the problems themselves. And if people cannot use it simply to say a problem exists then this may deter staff from reporting problems to which they personally have no answer. Yet, as a manager, you need to know about these too.

If staff are to be encouraged to spot and report problems even though they have no idea how to solve them, then a different approach is needed. One way is to stock each work area with an ample supply of forms on which staff can notify such problems. The forms need to stress that you need to know what the problems are, even if no solutions are offered. Once you know of a problem you may find that you have a solution yourself (or know someone else who might have). Alternatively (and if the size of the problem warrants it), you might set up a working party, Quality Circle or Error Correction Team to investigate the issue and propose solutions. These are discussed in more detail in a later chapter.

If you can meet your staff face to face, then team briefing meetings in which the team brief *you* (as well as the other way round) can work well – as long as the communication really is two-way. Other direct ways of consulting range from formal advisory team meetings to informal methods such as systematically and regularly asking about any problems during a customary walkabout. (But note the key words here: systematically and regularly.)

The method (or methods: you may need to use more than one) that you choose by which to consult your staff will depend on what suits you, your staff and your particular circumstances. What is important is that you do it – and that you act on it. Staff will soon lose faith in whatever system you choose (and in you) if they feel that their efforts to identify and notify problems and difficulties go unrewarded by any action. And don't just take action; make sure everyone knows you have – especially the person or people who brought the problem to your attention.

Finally, it's just as important to explain why you can't (or won't) take action on any issue. It's not always possible to solve a problem within the resources (time, money, skill) available to you and your staff: if so, tell them. They'll understand. And someone may just be prompted into suggesting a solution which hadn't occurred to you, and which you *could* implement.

55

## COLLABORATING

Whilst consulting is important it is not, on its own, sufficient. The empowering manager needs to go further. Full collaboration between managers and staff should be the ultimate goal of any empowerment programme. Only by collaborating freely, openly and fully can all the skills and knowledge within an organisation be harnessed towards its goals.

It's also the ultimate test not just of a manager's skill in empowerment, but of the *will* to implement it fully. The ability to regard staff as being every bit as important to the organisation's or department's goals as you are, and to treat them accordingly, is essential in any empowering manager. This requires the ability to see staff as full – not just junior – partners in the organisation's enterprise. This has implications for various aspects of the work of the organisation or department. For example, if all staff are to be regarded as full partners, who will call and run meetings? Clearly, if real collaboration is to happen, then all staff need to feel that they can set up meetings if need be, and run them too. Obviously this will require co-ordination, but unless staff feel they can act directly in this way to address issues or discuss ideas, then empowerment has not been achieved.

Some managers may feel that the last thing anyone needs is more meetings, and few would argue with that. In practice, therefore, it is unlikely that such a change will actually result in substantially more meetings overall, at least once an initial small flurry has died down. The team as a whole is perfectly capable of deciding which meetings are likely to prove productive and worthwhile and which are not. Working together to decide on this could be a useful first step towards collaboration.

At a different level, if all are to be seen as equal partners in the enterprise, who is to make strategic decisions? At first sight it would seem impossible to give everyone within an organisation an equal say in how an organisation should be run and what its products and markets should be. Yet some organisations – co-operatives – actually work in just this way, and another model exists in the power that company shareholders have. So the idea is less outlandish than it might appear. In practice, full membership at most levels within the organisation will be within team or department, and full collaboration is certainly possible in such smaller units. But does this rob the managers of such teams or departments of their strategic responsibilities? Not at all. As a manager your skills at identifying goals and developing strategy are more necessary than ever. Indeed, one main benefit of empowerment – and a major reason for endeavouring to put it into practice – is that it frees the manager to concentrate on strategic issues rather than being enmeshed in time-consuming tasks such as taking trivial decisions which others could take, and fighting fires which could be avoided.

In fact, it is essential that the empowering manager is able to offer a strategic perspective to what staff do if they are to understand the importance of their work to the goals of the organisation. Without such a strategic perspective, lower-level work, in particular, can seem pointless and uninspiring. If staff can be helped to see the relevance of their tasks to the success of the organisation, then both motivation and standards of work will increase. Such a perspective can also help all the members of a team or department to recognise and respect one another's different tasks and roles.

Nor does collaboration mean that a manager will no longer to be able to initiate strategic change. Implementing any kind of strategic change has always required that managers achieve staff acceptance of, or at least compliance with, the idea. Collaboration actually offers a more effective way to do that. Without the full and wholehearted involvement of your staff any major strategic change will falter, and may fail. If, however, staff feel they have been fully involved in the decision, then their endorsement is much more likely to be committed and enthusiastic than if ideas are simply imposed on them. Collaborative discussion of proposed changes actually makes their success more, not less, likely. What's more, if you can't persuade your staff that your idea is a good one then it may be worth listening carefully to their reservations: they may just have a point. Perhaps a joint, collaborative re-assessment might produce a better solution. And, of course, even if they do concur with your proposals, they may have useful additional ideas and suggestions to make.

57

Collaboration needn't mean that the manager loses the strategic role, and it may help to ensure that strategic change is thought through rather better than would otherwise have been the case. It will also help to ensure success of the strategic change once it is implemented.

So, should a manager who wishes to introduce empowerment to the organisation or department work collaboratively with staff to plan its implementation? Certainly! But if your organisation is not already some way along the road to empowerment there may need to be some preparatory work before staff are able – or even willing – to work in this way. They may need some preliminary training, and so might you. Collaboration is a skill, like any other, and you and your staff might benefit from training together, learning collaborative ways of working. The empowerment techniques discussed in a later chapter offer one way of introducing collaborative working. Working together to learn how to use them might be an excellent start, provided you are sure you will be able to avoid playing the dominant role in the process. If you're not sure you could avoid this trap (and it's an easy one to fall into: staff may even try to push you), then an external facilitator or trainer would be a sound idea and a worthwhile investment. Another approach would be a suitable course in team-working, though you need to beware of those which stress such things as leadership, etc. They may not be suitable for organisations which are attempting to empower, and may even be counter-productive.

But however you introduce the idea, collaboration is a skill which develops with practice. The more you try to work in this way the better you and your staff will become at it, especially if you can learn to forgive one another's early mistakes. So, start as soon as you can, and you will have taken an important early step towards true empowerment.

58

## MENTORING

Mentoring is as much a life stage as a management technique. In our early careers we typically want to do everything personally. We want to be in the thick of the action, spotting the problems and providing the solutions ourselves. Later, with greater maturity and experience, we may come to realise that we can actually achieve more and extend our sphere of influence by working through others, rather than attempting to do it all directly ourselves. We may prefer to pass on what we have learned rather than continue to apply our skill and knowledge directly. This gives us a wider canvas to work on than that within our personal sphere of influence: we can actually achieve more this way than by trying to do it all ourselves. This process is called mentoring: acting as both a role model and coach for staff and colleagues. It goes beyond delegation and is fundamental to the process of empowerment: until you can fully accept that you *don't* have to do it all yourself – and that you can achieve more by working through others – you will not be ready to empower your staff to take action for themselves.

In empowerment, the most important kind of role model you can be is, of course, a self-empowered manager. Unless staff see that you are prepared to take risks and extend the boundaries of your role then they are hardly likely to want to do the same. You also need to 'walk the talk'. All your interactions with your staff should support the idea that empowerment is both possible and desirable. They need to see you showing both enthusiasm in the idea and confidence in them (as well as in yourself).

Similarly, coaching is an essential aspect of mentoring. We have seen how important it is to recognise the skills and knowledge that your staff possess. It's equally important to recognise your own and to make sure that you pass these on to your staff. Knowledge isn't just power. It's the fuel that empowerment runs on. You need to make sure that you make your own skills and knowledge available on a wider basis.

59

We've seen, too, how important staff training is in empowerment. But training needn't always consist of expensive courses. Passing on your knowledge and skills by coaching your staff – and encouraging them to coach one another – is both an effective and economical approach. Of course it can never totally replace formal training: you'll always need to include some of that in your staff training programme to ensure an inflow of new ideas and approaches. But it is an excellent way to ensure that hard-won expertise is shared and not locked inside one head or pair of hands.

Mentoring, however, goes beyond either of these. The successful mentor will also wish to help staff grow and develop, just as the mentor has done.

## Growing your staff

The 'old' style of manager occupied an essentially parental role towards staff, treating them rather as a father or mother might.

Sometimes the manager was a stern and suspicious 'parent', carefully checking on the children's every move, expecting total compliance with a plethora of rules, severely punishing any breach of these rules, and keeping an ever-watchful eye at all times to spot misdemeanours. Sometimes, however, the manager was a benevolent parent, always willing to listen to their 'children's' problems, being caring, setting few rules as long as the 'children' behaved reasonably, and reacting more with sorrow and disappointment than with anger if rules were broken or errors made. But whether benevolent or despotic, the role was essentially still that of a parent towards a child.

Of course, staff also played their part in this little drama, taking on the role of child. Some staff naturally tend towards the 'good girl/boy' role, the apple of the parent/manager's eye. Others are rebellious, taking pleasure in breaking rules, or at least bending them as far as possible whilst getting away with it. Still others tend to fall into the sulky teenager role, more or less sticking to the rules, but in a half-hearted and reluctant manner, tending to stick to the letter rather than the principle of the law, rather than being wholehearted and cheerful in their acceptance of it. No wonder some managers are reluctant to empower their staff: they secretly see them at best as sulky adolescents, or even as downright children.

But this is no way to for grown adults to deal with one another. You are not a parent to your staff (even if on the whole they are many years younger than you) and they are not your children. You need to relate to them – and they to you – as adult to adult. Not only will you then feel confident that they will deal well with empowerment in the workplace, but *they* will feel confident to cope with it too. But how can you move out of your parental role into an adult-to-adult one? In much the same way that parents of growing children do: you need to help your staff to 'grow up'.

This will be essential if you are to achieve true empowerment, but may not be as easy as might first appear. The fact is that many staff essentially *like* their child-to-parent role. If they are 'good' children they are praised, and perhaps even promoted. If they are rebels/naughty children they get a sense of adventure, of being beyond 'parental' control, the romantic 'wild outlaw' of the department. And sulky teenagers – like sulky teenagers everywhere – are free to moan and groan, secure in the knowledge that they can rely on you to make sure they're looked after, whilst retaining the right to criticise you (and their 'brothers' and 'sisters') as and when they please. What's more they can, just like teenagers, demand at one minute that you leave them to make their own decisions and stop checking on them, then the next moment demand that *you* should take responsibility for something they are fearful of coping with alone.

But no matter what kind of 'children' your staff might be, the benefits to them are the same: freedom from ultimate responsibility. You as their parent/manager carry that! But in a truly empowered organisation all share responsibility for achieving success. You need to help your staff grow into full adult self-direction at work. So how can you and your staff move away from these parent/child roles towards those of the adults-working-with-adults that you actually are?

61

The answer isn't necessarily that easy. Many people are reluctant to take on responsibility. Why? Because they are frightened of being blamed if anything goes wrong. When people say 'I don't want the responsibility', what they usually really mean is 'I don't want to risk failing.' That's why this book places so much emphasis on the need to engender a climate of trust. Remove the fear of failure – or, rather, fear of the unpleasant consequences of failure – and you will have gone a long way towards removing the fear of responsibility.

You also need to ensure that goals and objectives are clear. Few things sap staff's confidence in themselves as much as lack of clarity about what is expected of them. But they need more than that. They need, too, to know where the boundaries of their responsibilities are.

If your staff are accustomed to seeing and dealing with you as their manager in a quasi-parental role, then you may need to take a leaf out of the book of successful parents if you are to help your staff to 'grow up' as quickly, painlessly and healthily as possible. Like a sensible and sensitive parent, you will help your growing 'children' by negotiating – not imposing – rules and boundaries. Then you will gradually relax the rules and extend the boundaries as the 'children' become more independent of you and more confident in their ability to cope. You'll make sure that they develop the knowledge, skills and understanding they will need to take sensible independent decisions. And you'll recognise that they – and you – need to have the courage to take a few sensible risks from time to time.

This is often the hardest part of parenting – and of empowering too. Recognising and accepting the need to let go, to allow children/staff to make their own mistakes and learn from them will always be difficult. It's hard, too, to see someone struggling to cope with a task that we ourselves would find easy. But just as children must learn to cross roads and tie their own shoelaces, so staff must learn to risk making their own decisions within a specified area of accountability without always seeking your advice or permission. And they must also learn to manage tasks which you have previously found it easier to handle yourself. Of course it's quicker and simpler for a parent to tie a child's shoelaces rather than wait patiently while the child struggles. But if the child is ever to cope alone, the parents must learn to grit their teeth and stand back.

The rewards of successful empowerment are also similar to those of successful parenting: seeing someone grow from nervousness and self-doubt into a confident, independent, and largely self-managing individual. And as with successful parents, each small step towards independence will gradually reduce the demands made on you. This is the key issue: imagine what you could do if you no longer had to manage your staff because they were perfectly capable of managing themselves. What might you do with this new-found freedom? Perhaps you could finally stop fire-fighting and start to think more strategically about the direction your organisation or department ought to be taking in future. And isn't that a better use of your management skills?

## Supporting

Of course, all good managers recognise the need to support their staff as well as help them become independent. In fact, neglected children – or unsupported staff – seldom grow up to be fully capable adults. But empowerment requires another dimension to be added to general support staff commonly receive from their managers: support when they make errors. The central importance of this was discussed in the previous chapter and emphasised again earlier, but it can hardly be stressed too often. If your staff don't feel that they will still enjoy your wholehearted support even if they make a mistake – provided that the mistake was made as a result of trying to meet organisational goals – then your organisation or department will never achieve full empowerment, and all the benefits this brings.

63

The real impact of empowerment comes when managers begin to see giving the right kind of support as their primary role, ahead of traditional leadership and certainly ahead of control. Remember that inverted pyramid. In that view of management, the manager is no longer at the top of the pile supported *by* his or her staff, but playing a supporting role to those staff by facilitating, consulting, coaching and mentoring them so that they are enabled to reach the organisation's goals for service and productivity.

# Leading from behind

Managing an inverted pyramid requires a management style which is very different from the traditional one which stresses leadership and control. We've examined some of the skills this needs. Yet, whilst the inverted pyramid is a useful picture to have, helping us to see that the traditional shape of an organisation needn't prevent empowerment – providing we look at it the right way – it is essentially a static picture. We need another image which stresses the dynamic nature of the task of management.

Such a picture does exist, but in a rather unexpected place. It can be found in the management style of a very different group of people from most managers and their staff: army generals and their troops. If we look at the essential role played by the empowering manager, we see that in many ways it's not so new at all. It's actually very similar to the role occupied by generals in times of war: leading from behind. Successful generals seldom lead from the front (unless they have the urge to be seen as heroes). They do, however, spend a lot of time and energy setting objectives and planning the strategy by which these will be reached. Then they make sure that their front-line troops know what is required of them and let them get on with it. And they don't expect to be consulted over every little decision that those troops have to make in order to achieve those objectives.

The main difference between the empowering manager and a general is that the manager will consult the 'troops' before planning any campaign. Of course generals take soundings to find out whether their plan is operationally feasible and likely to be successful. But the empowering manager will want to consult all the front-line troops, not just the 'officers' (other managers, supervisors, etc.), before setting goals and planning strategy. The results of these consultations will have a major effect on the resulting goals, strategies and plans for the organisation or department.

Like a general, then, the empowering manager leads from behind. Unlike a general, though, he or she recognises the skills and front-line knowledge which the 'troops' possess and understands the importance of accessing and harnessing these if the organisation is to achieve its goals.

# 5

# The empowering manager

otal Quality Management (TQM) was a popular management strategy in the 1980s. You may have been involved in – or perhaps instigated – a TQM programme within your organisation. If you have, you may well have come to wonder why it failed to deliver all that it seemed to promise. You were told that it would reduce errors and waste and improve customer service. You were led to believe that staff performance would improve and that morale would increase too. You were persuaded that it was essential to focus on Quality if the organisation was to be competitive and survive.

And it *should* have worked. The idea is good. The techniques are sound. Yet what I consistently hear from managers in organisations, large and small, in both the private and the public sector, is that in too many instances TQM has failed to achieve all that it should – and could – have done.

But why has TQM failed to live up to expectations? Why does it now have such a bad name in some quarters that companies are already abandoning it, or revamping it as 'continuous improvement' and so on. Why? Because it focused on production and processes, and not on the people who operate them. And because managers failed to realise that you can't just change the systems and procedures: you have to change the culture too.

In too many organisations TQM became seen by staff as just another device for controlling people and their outputs, not for enabling them to do their best. Staff at all levels became cynical and resistant as they came to see TQM as a way to restrict their autonomy rather than liberate their abilities. In the UK, at least, it has typically been initiated in a watered-down form without any substantial attempts to change attitudes. It was seen as a bolt-on extra rather than the major cultural upheaval it needed to be if it were to succeed fully.

Of course organisations introducing TQM tried to 'sell' the scheme to their staff, persuading them of the organisational and commercial benefits TQM could bring. They trained some staff in the concepts of TQM (though fewer received any training in applying TQM techniques). But where was the bulk of this educational and training effort most frequently expended? At senior management levels. Most UK organisations attempting to introduce TQM over the last few years seem to have taken the injunction to ensure that TQM has commitment at the top in a way that was both too literal and too limited. They concentrated their efforts at the top of the organisation. Only slowly and gradually did they begin to 'cascade' the ideas down through the levels until it reached the key level in the organisation: the front-line staff. All too often, however, by the time it reached these staff, the cascade had become a trickle – and a pretty meagre one at that.

Of course, top-level commitment is essential if TQM is to succeed. But bottom-level commitment is every bit as important too. Yet front-line staff were often the last to be involved. Worse, by the time they did come to be formally introduced to the ideas behind TQM, they had already heard too much about it via the usual 'jungle telegraph'.

As we all know, the jungle telegraph (which operates so much more quickly than formal communication systems in most organisations) is typically both inaccurate and pessimistic. By the time operative staff came to hear much about the ideas of TQM they had already decided that it was just another way to restrict their independence and check up on their failures. They were resistant to the idea from the start. What is worse, too few of them seem to have been given any substantial opportunity to become involved in the TQM process. Their involvement was often limited to being exhorted via posters and so on to remember the Quality messages the company put out. Only rarely, it seems, did organisations truly involve operative-level staff in any direct action aimed at tapping their skills and knowledge to improve the Quality of the product, process or service.

Yet in some organisations real cultural change *has* happened, and staff at all levels have become involved in – and therefore committed to – active endeavours to improve Quality. In these organisations every single member of staff has the opportunity to become involved in activities such as belonging to Error Correction Teams, using TQM techniques to solve problems in their section or department, or training peers to use such techniques. Organisations like these tend to have much more success with TQM and do achieve many of the savings and improvements it promises.

67

Why is it then that some organisations succeed in implementing TQM by really involving staff at all levels so that they actually do achieve substantial results when others do not? Because, in organisations where TQM has not delivered the promised results, their TQM programmes are still based on an outmoded and inappropriate view of people and their capabilities.

# Theories X, Y and Z

In the 1950s, the well-known management writer Douglas McGregor identified two basic views that management hold about the staff in their organisations. He called these views Theory X and Theory Y. All managers, he says, tend to hold one or other of these contrasting views about human nature in organisations, and the view they hold affects the way they manage their staff.

What kind of manager are you: Theory X or Theory Y? Read the pairs of statements overleaf and decide which one of each pair you agree with more.

a1) It's important to keep a careful eye on staff at all times because if you don't they tend to become sloppy in their work, and don't work as hard as they could.

a2) Once staff know exactly what's expected of them it's best just to let them get on with it without close supervision: they'll work harder and better without being checked all the time.

b1) I get my best results by being firm with my staff.

b2) I get my best results by being kind to my staff.

c1) On the whole, people don't want responsibility and will avoid it if they can.

c2) On the whole, people could handle more responsibility than they are given and would like more.

d1) Most people – given the chance – will do as little as possible, and need to be bribed or persuaded to do their best.

d2) Most people – given the chance – enjoy working hard and just need to be encouraged to do their best.

e1) The most important tools in managing people are objectives, control and standards.

e2) The most important tools in managing people are encouragement, support and delegation.

If you chose mainly 1s, you probably tend to hold the Theory X view of people and employees. If you chose mainly 2s, you probably tend to hold the Theory Y view.

Managers who hold Theory X views about staff typically regard people as being naturally lazy and not inclined to do any work at all unless goaded or bribed. The Theory X manager assumes that staff lack ambition and avoid responsibility, preferring to be led by others. Further, such managers see staff as fundamentally self-centred and without any real interest in the organisation or its goals. Theory X managers therefore tend towards a management style in which the manager's prime task is seen as being the organisation of resources. Staff resources are directed and controlled by using persuasion, coercion, rewards and punishments to modify people's behaviour till it fits organisational requirements.

Theory Y managers, on the other hand, believe that if people seem passive and lacking in responsiveness to the organisation's needs, they have become so as a result of working in organisations which fail to recognise their capacity to take on responsibility. Theory Y managers see staff as having both the motivation and the potential to align their behaviour to organisational goals if managers make it possible for them to do so. The prime task of managers is to set conditions so that people can achieve their own goals by working to achieve organisational objectives.

Having read this far, you will have recognised that Theory Y is more appropriate then Theory X to both TQM and empowerment. But most managers to whom I have given the checklist you completed earlier without first explaining what it is about tend to tick 1s rather than 2s. This leads me to suppose that Theory X is still the dominant view of people in organisations in the UK today. Small wonder, then, that TQM has failed to live up to expectations. In many organisations it didn't stand a chance.

Though Theory X still persists so widely it is no longer appropriate in any organisation, let alone one attempting to introduce either TQM or empowerment. It may have been an appropriate view of staff in the past when managers and staff were drawn from different social classes and educational systems. But nowadays people at all levels in organisations are better trained and educated than ever before and much more able to make an effective contribution within any organisation. We also inhabit a much less formal world, in which people are less willing to accept overt control than in the past (also, perhaps, because of narrowing educational and class differences). Theory X is quite simply outmoded, inappropriate and ineffective as a management theory with which to approach the relatively sophisticated and well-informed workforces of today.

Yet Theory Y is not enough either. The empowering manager needs a new kind of theory which goes beyond even that. In practice, I find, managers who identify themselves with Theory Y on the checklist above may have a more optimistic view of people and their capabilities than Theory X managers, but they still tend to place themselves at the top of the hierarchy, and in the driving seat. Theirs may be a more benevolent view of the process of management but it is still an essentially paternalistic one. They may be less controlling and suspicious than those managers who identify with Theory X beliefs, but they still tend to regard their role as being to lead whilst staff follow. But true empowerment depends on treating staff with respect as intelligent adults who need support, not leadership, to achieve success at work.

People are perfectly capable of making their own decisions outside their working environment. They run their families and get on with their lives remarkably well despite the lack of a benevolent manager directing and leading them. Often, as Tom Peters has pointed out, people hold down positions of substantial responsibility as voluntary workers or within their own fields of interest outside their working hours.

Your staff may be running local voluntary organisations, setting up sports leagues, raising large sums of money for charity, even serving on political committees or councils, all in their spare time. Isn't it rather odd, then, that we feel they have to be regulated with such care and given strong leadership when they are at work? On the whole, people cope perfectly well with the empowerment they exercise and enjoy in everyday life. Yet we somehow contrive to ignore these skills and experience when they come to work.

What empowering managers need is a theory which focuses on what managers must do to recognise and harness the full range of abilities and knowledge which staff could bring to work if only we would let them. We need a theory which encompasses awareness of the need to facilitate rather than command, to support rather than lead (at least in the conventional sense). One such theory, Theory Z, is said by Japanese management theorist W. Ouchi to offer a new philosophy of management. Coined to give a name to the attempts by Western organisations to adapt Japanese management practice to Western needs, Theory Z stresses the need to share decision-making and reduce artificial status barriers between workers and management. It stresses the need for improved communications and greater individual responsibility for work outcomes, as well as greater recognition for the individual's contribution to the team. Ouchi emphasises that people, not technology, must be co-ordinated to achieve organisational aims.

Yet much of the success of such approaches in Japan is due to cultural factors which are less common in the UK. Japanese management practice, on which Theory Z is based, works best in a context which offers lifetime job security, and in which the importance of group allegiance and the acceptance of collective responsibility are strong national characteristics. In practice, Japanese companies operating in the West have had to modify some of their traditional approaches to take account of Western culture. In particular, the strongly individualist nature of Western culture has made many of the collectivist approaches common in Japan difficult to import wholesale.

It might also be argued that where Japanese companies have been successful in persuading Western staff to adopt unfamiliar approaches this has largely happened in areas of very high unemployment where alternative jobs are scarce or non-existent. Whether employee acceptance of some of the more formal and rigid aspects of Japanese management style is more than skin deep is not clear. In particular, it is by no means certain that the level of regulation of behaviour – often by the strong imposition of group norms of behaviour and expression – which is also typical of Japanese companies would be acceptable in a Western-owned company. Nor is it clear to what extent employees in such companies accept such conditions and systems precisely because the company is *not* Western and they therefore accept the need to adopt a different approach just as they would if they were actually working in another country.

71

What is likely, however, is that non-Japanese organisations are unlikely to be successful in attempting the wholesale adoption of Japanese methods no matter how successful they may be in Japan, or in Japanese-owned companies outside Japan. Western societies are both less formal and less group-oriented than Japanese society. UK society tends to stress individual needs rather than group goals, and whilst we may have much to learn about placing greater emphasis on collective aims and successes it is unrealistic to suppose that we can force entire workforces to adopt an unfamiliar cultural attitude to order simply to increase business success.

There are also dangers associated with the kind of group-dependent, high-success-oriented culture to be found in Japan. Undue emphasis on team needs and team successes may result in neglect of the individual goals and personal achievements which may be more motivating for some people, especially in Western society. It may also lead to a kind of imprisonment of the will and of individual initiative as the group seeks to prevent any dissent, or even questioning, which may undermine its cohesiveness. Organisations actually need some mavericks, individuals who can stand outside group norms and bring a fresh perspective to bear on issues and problems.

The uncritical and wholesale adoption of Japanese management methods should therefore be approached with caution. Certainly the West has much to learn from Japanese management systems and approaches. Equally, however, we in the UK need to recognise the potential strengths of our own culture – particularly its acceptance of the value of non-conformity and of individual needs – if we are to move forward to a new approach to management which synthesises the best of each into a strategy which is appropriate for Western culture. We need a new theory of management to support true empowerment of the individual as well as the group in the workplace: Theory E.

72

# The Theory E manager

Like Theory Y and Z managers, the Theory E manager believes people capable of more than most organisations allow them to contribute; and that people want to do a good job and will do so if you let them. However, the Theory E manager also believes that managers are more effective as facilitators than as leaders, and that they must devolve power – not just responsibility – to individuals as well as groups. The kind of devolution of power on which true empowerment depends goes beyond conventional delegation. Delegation merely *lends* responsibility – it can be taken back at any time – and retains real power at all times: the delegatee simply acts in place of the delegator. Devolution, however, is permanent and includes power as well as responsibility: the person to whom a role or task is devolved becomes wholly responsible for it in his or her own right. In other words, the Theory E manager believes in making people responsible *for*, not just responsible *to*.

Above all, the Theory E manager believes that belief is not enough: action is required to ensure that true empowerment happens.

# The eight Es of empowerment

It's no good simply saying what the empowering manager's attitudes and beliefs need to be. The empowering manager also needs to know what to do. Practical implementation will be discussed in later chapters, but what follows is a list of important precepts to guide the empowering manager. These are the rules or canons of successful empowerment, no matter what your personal situation and no matter what adaptions you may need to make to fit empowerment to your particular organisational circumstances.

## ENVISION

How do you ensure that devolution doesn't become revolution?

The first requirement is a shared vision so that staff know what the entire organisation or department is striving towards. They need to have a clear picture of what is wanted – and why. If everyone is clear about the aims of the organisation or department then activity can be largely self-co-ordinating. If you and your staff are clear about ends, then means can be left to individuals to decide, provided certain parameters are set.

You need to work with your staff to develop a clear, shared vision of what you want to achieve. Then you can agree specific goals and objectives for both individuals and groups, and set clear boundaries around areas of devolved power. Once people know what they and others are working towards it becomes possible to co-ordinate effort and the use of resources much more efficiently and amicably. Most squabbles over resources or clashes of activities in organisations are the result of confused or conflicting goals. Establish a clear *shared* vision which emphasises priorities, common goals and collaboration – not competition – and such problems can be largely avoided.

## EDUCATE

Staff need to understand *why* as well as know *what* if they are to make sensible decisions. This requires education, not just training. This is by no means the trivial distinction it may at first appear to be. The difference between the two is profound and important.

Training aims to standardise behaviour, to ensure that staff will behave reliably and consistently in a given, predictable set of circumstances. Education, on the other hand, understands that it is neither possible nor desirable to attempt to control behaviour in all circumstances and at all times. Education accepts that there will be occasions on which staff will have to exercise their own judgement and make their own decisions about what should be done. It therefore aims to make behaviour unpredictable in detail, but appropriate and effective to the context in which it occurs, by ensuring that people understand an underlying set of rules or principles, *and* the reasons for these.

Training in specific skills will, of course, continue to be necessary. But true empowerment requires staff to be able to make independent decisions which may vary depending on circumstances. That requires education. Share your vision of success and ensure that staff understand why it is important and what the goals are. Then they will be able to take sensible decisions and calculated risks for themselves based on a solid grasp of the essentials.

## ELIMINATE

The empowering manager needs to strive to eliminate all barriers to empowerment. First and foremost this means ensuring that all organisational systems and procedures are aligned with the goals of the organisation and with empowerment as the process by which these will be achieved. Eliminate any unnecessary rules or regulations which stand in the way of empowerment. Remove obstacles and barriers of all kinds, whether human, administrative or technical.

And yes, this may mean moving people who cannot adjust to the need for empowerment. If retraining or persuasion doesn't work it may be necessary to move individuals who are acting as blocks to progress to a less influential position. In extreme cases they may have to leave the organisation or department. But in most cases both individual and collective resistance to empowerment can be overcome. This will be discussed in a later chapter. Often, too, systems and procedures need to be reassessed. Chapter 4 discussed some ways in which you might do this. But most often the real barriers to empowerment are not individuals or organisational procedures but negative personal attitudes, including your own.

Personal attitudes of your own which you may need to strive to eliminate include a punitive attitude to errors and a low evaluation of staff abilities. If you respond harshly to errors and have doubts about staff capabilities you will never achieve true empowerment in your organisation or department. A more positive – and actually more realistic – attitude is needed. Keep reminding yourself of how much more you are capable of (and all those mistakes you have made which have contributed to your present levels of skill and understanding) and you will come to expect more achievement (and less perfection) of your staff too.

---

Your belief in what your staff can achieve may be a more powerful factor than you realise. Some years ago educational researchers who were interested in the way teachers' expectations affected pupil performance carried out an experiment at a primary school. They tested all the children's IQs, and assessed their achievements to date. They then told teachers that their results had shown that certain children were due to make extra-fast progress and that teachers should expect to see particularly large gains in achievement from these specific pupils. The researchers then left.

Some months later they returned to the school. The children they had identified had indeed progressed much faster than their peers. It was only then that the researchers revealed the truth. These children had, in fact, been selected purely at random. There was no reason at all to believe that they actually would make faster progress than their peers, yet they did. Why? Because their teachers expected them to.

---

Eliminate any low expectations you may have about your staff's abilities to cope with empowerment and you may be astonished at what you and they can achieve together. You also need to eliminate any negative attitudes which staff themselves hold, especially a low evaluation of their own and colleagues' abilities. Find ways to convey your confidence in your staff, and your conviction that they will be able to cope with the new opportunities and demands of empowerment. Similarly, you need to encourage staff to value one another's individual strengths and abilities.

One important aspect of this is the elimination of unnecessary and inappropriate internal competition. This means above all that promotion and staff development criteria have to be open and fair. If staff feel they must constantly compete with one another for promotion or bonuses, without any clear sense of the basis on which judgements will be made about them, then there will always be a tendency to criticise others and fail to offer them support when needed. The criteria on which staff performance is to be judged must be open for all to see.

Openness, however, is not enough. Too often there is indeed a set of explicit, rational, fair criteria, open to all to see and clearly related to observable performance. But these open criteria bear no apparent resemblance to the real criteria, which seem to be based on a mixture of patronage and prejudice. This is no basis for mutual support and encouragement between staff. If you are to eliminate negative attitudes between staff, each individual must feel that supporting others will enhance rather than jeopardised his or her position. In addition to being open, fair and real, the promotion and bonus criteria need to address this issue directly too.

77

You might consider including within your performance assessment criteria some measures of interpersonal support and encouragement. Staff need to see that the success of an individual is also success for the team (the reverse of the 'team as hero' Japanese-influenced approach) and that their own chances of progress and individual success are not threatened by the success of others. Then they are more likely to recognise one another's strengths, and to offer support in helping to overcome weaknesses rather than try to capitalise upon them for personal gain.

And, of course, as will be stressed again and again, you need to eliminate the fear of your criticism following failure. It is essential that staff come to realise that it's just as important to do the right thing under varying circumstances as it is to do things right in predictable ones. They need to feel that whilst you will accept genuine error, what you *will* always criticise is inertia and the failure to try.

## EXPRESS

No matter how convinced you may be of the need for

empowerment, you can't expect your staff to feel the same keenness unless they, too, understand what it is about. You must be prepared to explain not just what empowerment is, but what benefits it can bring to them as individuals, as well as to the organisation or department. But more than that, you need to be clear about goals and directions. Staff need to know *why* what is wanted, is wanted. Don't follow the example of the multinational organisation about whose empowerment programme one former manager told me: 'My boss simply came in one morning and said, "As of today, you're empowered." I said, "Empowered to do what?" He didn't seem to know. And that was it! I never did know what it was supposed to mean.'

Most important of all is the need to express your own personal views and opinions clearly and honestly. There can be no real empowerment where staff feel they have to keep trying to second-guess what you want, think and believe. That only breeds anxiety and insecurity. People need to know where they – and you – stand if they are to feel confident enough to use their initiative and try to extend the boundaries of what they can do. So express your personal views clearly. Don't keep staff guessing what it is you want. Most important of all, don't keep them guessing about how they, you or the organisation or department is doing. We all need open, honest feedback about our performance if we are to be able to make any necessary improvements.

You also need to let staff know if you think they're making mistakes. Empowerment doesn't mean letting people sink or swim purely by their own efforts. If you think people are on the wrong track *tell* them so. But resist the temptation to take over and run things yourself. Remember: delegation is temporary, but devolution is permanent. Staff will never feel secure enough to exercise initiative if they feel under constant threat that you may snatch power back at any time.

You must be able to engage in honest, open dialogue about your concerns in a way which makes these clear but which also allows others to explain their own thinking. After all, they may be right.

It won't be easy at first. You will find it hard to strike the right balance between offering no-strings advice based on legitimate concern and the urge to take over and run things as you see fit. Your staff will find it hard to get the right balance between being able to admit to problems and worries and trying to go it alone when they really should ask for help. But over time, and with effort on both sides, you should be able to arrive at a situation in which staff feel they can trust you to offer non-interfering support, and you feel you can trust them to admit when things are getting difficult – and before they get out of hand.

Be open about your own doubts and fears about the empowerment process itself. It won't always be plain sailing, and staff need to know this too. Otherwise, any small early setbacks may come to seem to be major problems which threaten the whole enterprise. They will have their doubts and fears about empowerment from time to time. It's essential that they understand that you feel these too. Then empowerment can become the joint venture it needs to be if it is to be successful.

Successful empowerment will also depend to a very large extent on the reduction in social distance between you and your staff. This has important implications and consequences. If you are truly to empower, rather than merely delegate, you cannot expect to remain in the power role, or retreat to it if the going gets tough. You need to be able to relinquish the role and the power at the same time. One consequence of this is that your own decisions and actions need to become as open to the scrutiny of your staff as theirs have always been to you. Of course they will always have judged and criticised your decisions, but even if you have been aware of this you will probably not have had to acknowledge it formally, or involve yourself in the process. Yet if staff are to be truly empowered, then part of that empowerment must be the power to criticise your decisions and actions directly and to ask for an explanation of them. This means that you will need to be prepared to express your own ideas and thinking clearly, openly and honestly. Your staff deserve to know not just what you are planning and thinking, but the underlying reasons too. Then they will be able to assess these for themselves. If you can learn to trust them to respond sensibly and with open minds, explaining your thoughts as well as your actions, then you are likely to find that their trust in you – and your judgements – will increase too. Paradoxically, this will actually make it easier for you to win them round to your point of view should you ever feel you need to do so.

Finally, staff also need to be able to express points of view or opinions to you, as well as to one another. They need to feel free to voice ideas, opinions, fears and concerns in an atmosphere free from ridicule or censorious criticism. This includes feeling free to criticise your actions as well as those of colleagues. It certainly includes the need to feel free to criticise the idea of empowerment itself should they see fit to do so. For this to be possible, everyone must learn to criticise actions and decisions, and not the people who took them. People need to be able to concentrate on giving feedback and not on scoring points. This may require some formal training. It certainly needs some formal rules and a shared understanding about what is, and what is not, acceptable. You may find this is best achieved by using an external consultant to assist in training staff in the necessary skills. An experienced assertiveness trainer will be able to help you to distinguish appropriate and constructive ways to share feelings and give feedback. At the very least you should consider some self-training by reading one of the many helpful books to be found on the topic and sharing what you have learned with your staff.

## ENTHUSE

In addition to being open and honest about expressing any doubts and fears you may have about empowerment, you need to generate excitement about it. If you seem lukewarm or half-hearted about the process, then you can hardly expect others to be very keen on the idea. Empowerment can seem rather daunting to both managers and staff, yet its potential benefits are enormous. You and your staff need to concentrate on those benefits and not on any small worries or difficulties which may stand in your way.

Empowerment can offer real enjoyment as it unfolds, as well as offering substantial personal and organisational benefits. You need to recognise where this enjoyment might lie for you and convey it to your staff. Of course, you may not be ready yourself for empowerment. If you are not, your reservations and doubts will surely seep out and become visible to others. So are you really ready for the idea yourself?

To be an enthusiastic advocate of empowerment, you need to be able to enjoy helping staff to grow rather than controlling them efficiently. You need to be able to enjoy seeing them gain better results by working independently than they could if you were directing and controlling them. You also need to enjoy your new role, working as part of the team rather than leading it, and sharing the credit as well as the problems. More than that, you need to be able to get a real kick out of sharing your ideas with others, then seeing them, not you, carry them through to successful completion. Above all, you need to be able to enjoy sharing power as well as responsibility.

81

Your staff need to sense that, as well as enthusing about the benefits of empowerment, you are keen enough on the idea to be willing to put your own energies into making it work: then they'll be prepared to put their full energy in too. If they don't see you putting your full effort and commitment into empowerment it *can* begin to look as if you are merely trying to hive off the parts of your own job that you find difficult or boring. If you can convince them that the idea is more than simply a device to relieve you of some management pressure, then they are more likely to be enthusiasts for the idea too.

## EQUIP

Although empowering devolves power, the empowering manager retains responsibility for ensuring that staff have all they need and that the circumstances are right to ensure success. This means that the empowering manager needs to ensure that resource power is devolved too. You will need to make certain that your staff have the time, financial, physical and human resources they need to do the job. Without these there can be no true empowerment.

One of the most effective things you can do to empower your staff is to give them their own budget to control. Unless you are pre-pared to hand over the financial resources and responsibilities that go with any particular task or role, empowerment cannot happen. Hanging on to the budget sends a powerful signal that any empowerment is only skin-deep, and that you're not really serious in your intentions. The budget in question need not be large. Sometime all it takes is a few pounds to put someone firmly in the driving seat. Some retailing and service organisations have begun to authorise staff to spend whatever is necessary up to a specified sum to achieve customer satisfaction in the event of a complaint. Sums typically range from around £10 and upwards. Staff have absolute discretion over how and on whom such sums are spent (provided proper records are kept, of course).

For example, a customer who complains to a receptionist about the cleanliness of a hotel room may, in addition to being offered another room, be given a bottle of wine and some flowers by way of apology. The customer feels that the complaint was treated seriously and speedily, and the receptionist feels able to achieve a worthwhile result (and avoid a nasty scene too, perhaps) without having to seek special permission or refer the matter to a manager. Unless you anticipate large numbers of customer com-plaints (in which case you need to start by tackling them!) such a system need not be very costly, particularly when compared to the cost of losing a potential customer for life.

Conversely, exerting too tight a control over finances sends a powerful message of mistrust. Sometimes people still try to exercise such control even when budgets have been devolved. One company I know received an invoice for an inexpensive briefcase. The finance manager queried it, even though the briefcase had been ordered by an executive director of the company, to be paid for out of his departmental budget. What sort of message did that send to even senior managers about exercising their own discretion over their own budgets? How easy would it be for managers in that organisation to devolve a budget to their staff to control independently? In fact, the executive director concerned was actually rather good at empowering his own staff (thus showing that managers can overcome even the least promising circumstances), but the organisation was hardly encouraging him to do so. You need to negotiate sensible, fair budgets with your staff which will enable them to achieve the goals you have agreed with them. Then let them get on with spending their own budgets as they see fit.

In addition to financial and other more tangible resources, you will also need to ensure that your staff have sufficient skill, knowledge and confidence. This has obvious implications for training. You cannot expect people to react well to empowerment unless you provide them with the personal resources they need to do so. So set aside a training budget too, and make sure it's realistic. But remember that you may be able to achieve a great deal simply by sharing expertise and skills within the team. Remember, too, that staff's confidence in their ability to cope is only partly dependent on skills and knowledge. It also depends in large measure in how much confidence *you* have in them, and how well you convey this. If you really want to equip your staff to deal confidently with situations in an empowered organisation, then you need to show that you have confidence in them too. So tell them how much faith you have in them and their ability to cope, but bear in mind that a little praise goes a long way: too much can seem gushing and unconvincing.

83

## EVALUATE

Once the empowerment process is under way, it's essential to monitor progress and evaluate results. Empowerment is essentially a process, not an event, so monitoring and evaluation of it need to be a continuous and permanent feature of your management from now on. There should be two strands to the evaluation: your staff, and you.

You need to consider whether objectives and standards have been

- set
- met
- vet(ted)

and to assess how effective these objectives and standards have been in achieving your overall aims. This aspect of empowerment is discussed in greater depth in a later chapter.

What is important to stress here is that you and your management skills need to be evaluated too. And if you are serious about empowerment you need to involve your staff in this process. The idea of staff appraising their manager's performance is not new, though it is not yet very widespread. It is, however, gaining acceptance in organisations which wish to take the idea of staff empowerment seriously, for who else but your staff are in such a strong position to know how well you have accomplished the aims of empowerment?

Inviting staff to give you feedback on how you are doing can seem both threatening and questionable to some managers. Yet without it true empowerment cannot happen. If you devolve all power save that of appraisal and evaluation you have failed to empower fully. Unless staff have the same opportunity to comment on your performance as you have to comment on theirs, they cannot be said to have been empowered. In fact, though the idea can seem frightening to managers who are unused to it and who fear that staff will focus on the negatives and fail to give credit for the positives, staff rarely misuse or abuse the process. The real problem (as will be discussed later) is in finding ways to *enable* staff to feel safe enough to give negative feedback. And there can be a real boost to managers' confidence in hearing that their staff actually value what they do and how well they do it. It can somehow seem much more worthwhile than any amount of praise from above.

## EXPECT

Lastly, the empowering manager knows to expect some mistakes and teething troubles. Even the best-planned and managed empowerment programme is bound to have some flaws and hit some snags. So it's important to expect these, and even plan for them, to avoid being thrown off course by them. You will probably be unable to predict exactly when and why they will crop up (if you could, you could take steps to avoid them) but you can attempt to predict the *kind* of problems which might occur.

The kinds of problems which might occur depend on the organisation and its particular set of circumstances and staff. You need, therefore, to give some serious, conscientious thought to trying to identify where and why such problems might occur in your particular organisation and circumstances. It may be that you will lack support from above, or perhaps your staff will need some particular kind of training to help them.

One problem which is particularly likely to arise is staff resistance. You may find this surprising when it happens. You may see the potential benefits of empowerment so clearly that you find it hard to understand why any of your staff should wish to stay unempowered. (And the potential benefits for individuals as well as organisations are indeed great.) Yet staff may continue to resist even when these are pointed out to them. The reasons for this are complex, so this issue, together with ways of overcoming such resistance, is discussed in a later chapter. Suffice it to say here that you need to be prepared to encounter this and other kinds of problems.

Yet whatever pre-planning you do, there will almost certainly be other problems which you can't predict. But if you expect *some* problems to occur then you won't feel too daunted when they do. In fact, problems are a sign that you are actually making some headway: no problems may mean that no change has yet occurred. So expect them, and regard them as being fundamentally an encouraging sign. Overcome them and you have achieved real progress.

Finally, there is one other thing you ought to expect: success. If you can remain optimistic despite setbacks then success will come. Keep that thought firmly in mind and you and your staff will be able to ride out any small storms you may encounter on the way. If *you* remain confident of success then they will be confident too, and confidence, as we have seen, is an essential component of successful empowerment. So expect problems by all means, but expect success too, and it will become a self-fulfilling prophecy.

# 6

# Setting direction and maintaining control

**O**ne of the major anxieties which managers have when contemplating the introduction of empowerment in their organisation or department is the problem of maintaining sufficient
control to ensure that organisational objectives are achieved.
How, they wonder, can these be assured if staff are to be
empowered to make their own decisions and act on their own
initiative? Yet there really is no need for such anxiety for no real
conflict exists. Liberty is not the same as licence, and empowering
staff is by no means the same thing as dispensing with all goals,
objectives or performance measures.

In fact, successful empowerment depends more than ever on the
existence of goals and objectives. Managers fear that without
them there would be anarchy, with staff behaving as they please
in a chaotic free-for-all. In reality, what would happen is not
anarchy but stasis: nothing would happen because no one would
know what to do. Organisational paralysis – not turmoil – is what
actually happens when no clear goals exist. People become scared
to take any action beyond the mundane for fear of it being the
wrong thing to do. So nothing of substance is done. (How many
organisations does this describe? All too many, in my experience.)

## Setting goals

Clear goals are the key to organisational effectiveness, with or without empowerment, but in empowered organisations they become more important still. Specific, clear, shared goals are the chart by which everyone in the organisation steers, and against which all success is judged. Without the directions provided by such goals no progress would be possible.

But it is useless to vouchsafe these goals only to senior managers. That might work in unempowered organisations, in which managers control and direct all the activities of the workforce, who simply follow instructions (or fail to do so!). But in an empowered organisation it is essential that everyone should be aware of goals, and the priorities attached to them. Many organisations have recently attempted to align individual effort with organisational goals by writing and disseminating a mission statement, setting out what the organisation aims to do and how it wishes to do it. Some such attempts have been more successful than others.

88

The worst example I have come across so far was from a public sector organisation. It ran to three pages and nineteen separate aims, each up to a paragraph long! How on earth were the staff of that organisation to respond to that, even if they could remember any of it? How could they tell what the organisation's priorities were, and what theirs ought to be in response?

A mission statement which cannot be easily and quickly recalled by all staff is worse than useless. Worse because it brings into ridicule what could be a potentially useful organisational device.

A good mission statement needs to encapsulate neatly and briefly the organisation's major goal, or mission, in such a way that everyone within the organisation is provided with a simple statement to guide their actions, and against which they can be judged. Unfortunately, there is an inherent clash between the necessary brevity of a good mission statement, and the inclusion of a message of any real substance. What *can* be succinctly expressed in a short mission statement often turns out to be banal and uninspiring. In many cases all that really distinguishes them from the mission statements of competitors, is the organisation's name at the beginning.

So how can organisations communicate their goals in a way which both shapes and inspires staff activity? One way is through developing a shared vision.

## Creating a shared vision

A shared vision goes beyond a brief (or even lengthy) mission statement. It not only describes what an organisation wishes to achieve but what *kind* of organisation it wishes to be. A well-developed organisational vision encapsulates, verbally or visually, the organisation's aspirations as well as its intentions, and presents these in a form which is both individual and inspirational.

89

One Swedish company, Karmoy, has developed a company vision in the form of a highly inspirational picture. It has disseminated copies of it to all its staff, and displays it prominently throughout the workplace. The picture is painted in pleasing pastel colours, and shows flowers, birds and a bright sun. Not the obvious literal picture of a car company, perhaps, but one that clearly conveys the sense of harmony and optimism which is the company's aspiration for its workplace, and one that actually conveys far more to staff within the organisation than any trite and unstimulating mission statement (especially one three pages long!) could ever do.

This vision says little about *what* the organisation is trying to achieve, but speaks volumes about *how* it is trying to do it. In conjunction with a good, clear, brief mission statement, such a vision can add an important additional dimension to the work-force's understanding of what they are collectively striving for. It's an idea which can be as readily adapted for use by a department or team, as by an entire organisation, and one which is particularly suited to organisations, departments or teams where the manager wishes to introduce empowerment.

If you and your team or department are serious about implementing empowerment, then time spent developing a joint vision will be invaluable. Ways of developing an organisational or departmental vision are discussed in a later chapter. Use these to develop the right kind of vision for your organisation or department and to provide clearly expressed and shared goals, and you will have a powerful management tool to help you shape and guide staff endeavour.

## Exercising control

Some kind of control, however, remains essential. Someone has to ensure that activities stay in line with the shared vision and that endeavours are successful. The question is, does that someone always have to be you?

In traditional approaches to management, managers try to exercise tight control over both activities and outcomes. We have already seen, however, that such an approach is inappropriate today, and is likely to be counter-productive. Staff these days are likely to resent and react against over-zealous attempts to control what they do. What is required is an approach to management which ensures organisational success but which does so without imposing heavy management control over staff. One such approach has been described as 'loose-tight' management. The essence of the approach is that the manager retains tight control over setting objectives, but adopt a looser approach to the management of how these are achieved.

However, such tight managerial control over objectives seems inappropriate in a context of empowerment, in which staff are encouraged to contribute to the process of setting goals. What is needed in the empowered organisation is that *someone* should exercise tight control over objectives, but that person need not be the manager. Such control is more properly and effectively exercised by the person who 'owns' the objectives. Where group objectives exist, control, too, should be shared.

# Key tasks and personal objectives

We have become accustomed to the idea of identifying key tasks for individuals as part of the appraisal process. The better examples of job descriptions will usually include a list of such tasks also. Often, too, personal development objectives will be set at an appraisal interview, and employee progress will be monitored in terms of these. Yet few organisations take the small further step of regarding such key tasks and personal objectives as providing the necessary framework for *control* of organisational outcomes. The process is more often viewed simply as good practice in employee development than as part of organisational control. Perhaps that's why appraisal is so rarely done well.

The confusion has arisen partly because the proponents of appraisal have, quite rightly, been at pains to stress that effective appraisal should be about staff development, not promotion or rewards. They have hammered home the message that appraisal needs to be seen as a means to help employees improve their performance, not as an instrument for weeding out incompetence. They have repeatedly emphasised the need to separate appraisal from pay and promotion systems so that it can be an enabling rather than policing or assessing process. This is necessary if staff and managers are to feel safe enough to be open about performance, including any shortcomings. If appraisal is seen as evaluatory or critical, then staff are unlikely to be honest about any weaknesses or failings, and if these remain hidden no remedial action is possible.

Yet it is possible for a good appraisal system to be supportive and yet offer a means of control over performance and outcomes, if the individuals themselves (and not the manager) feel responsible for assessing performance and progress. The best appraisal systems do just this. A good system will try to ensure that personal objectives are aligned with departmental and organisational ones. It will also ensure that key tasks are similarly aligned. The manager retains responsibility for ensuring that the collective key tasks and objectives of his or her staff provide coherent and comprehensive coverage of the goals which will have to be reached if the organisation or department is to fulfil its mission.

If people are to be self-policing, it is essential that these key tasks and objectives should be set by a process of open negotiation between staff and managers. If staff are genuinely involved in discussing, negotiating and setting personal objectives and in defining their own key tasks, they then have not only the means to control their performance themselves but the will to do so.

## ALLOCATING KEY TASKS

As a manager you have an overview of all the tasks which need to be completed to achieve organisational goals. Staff may have a more limited view, but they may know more clearly their own abilities and interests. Setting key tasks, then, needs to be a joint process. You know what needs to be done. Staff know what they want to do. The result may be a neatly tailored fit or, more likely, a certain amount of compromise on both sides may be required. Staff may be much more willing to accept certain uncongenial roles or undesirable tasks if they feel that there is a quid pro quo for them in terms of being offered a desirable opportunity too. So before you begin to allocate tasks it's important to find out what staff already do, and what they want to do.

Start by looking at your own job description. How accurate is that? Whenever I ask managers this I tend to get a hollow laugh (unless the manager is very newly in post or the description has recently been rewritten). Most managers feel that any resemblance between their job description and what they actually do is sketchy at best. Yet they rarely carry this knowledge through to the realisation that their staff's job descriptions are likely to be equally misleading and inaccurate. So make a start by re-negotiating your own job description with your own line manager so that it is an accurate and useful guide to what you should be trying to do. Then turn your attention to the job descriptions of your staff.

Don't just assume that the job each individual is currently doing is the right one or that it makes the best use of his or her skills. One organisation I know well asks its key staff each year to complete a form detailing their current responsibilities and tasks, and what they would like them to be in the coming year. People are asked to indicate any relevant additional qualifications or experience they have gained since they last filled in such a form, and are given the opportunity to outline why they would like to move in any new direction, and what they might offer. The system grew up in a time of rapid expansion and change for the organisation, but it is every bit as pertinent at a time of consolidation or even stagnation. For many people a change is, indeed, as good as a rest, and rotating staff around so that they are able to learn and exercise new skills can be an important way to retain motivation and increase the total pool of staff skills and experience available to you as a manager.

Staff need to know, of course, that they may not be offered what they ask for. They also need to be able to trust you to take their suggestions seriously even if you are unable to meet them. So before you decide what people ought to be doing, ask them what they want to do. You may be surprised at some of the answers you receive. A job which strikes you as dull and repetitive may offer someone just the calm and undemanding tasks they feel most comfortable with. Similarly, a task which seems to you to offer an exiting challenge and the opportunity for advancement may seem terrifyingly complex and demanding to someone else. You may also find that staff have unfulfilled ambitions which you have never suspected.

A young, newly-appointed manager told me of the problems he was having with an older woman on his staff. She had worked in the organisation for a number of years, more or less running the department prior to his appointment (and been hoping for the job herself). She was not exactly obstructing him, but was certainly not smoothing his path. Talking to him, I suggested that he find some particular area of interest which she would like to be able to develop but had not so far had the opportunity to explore. He immediately realised that she had several times expressed an interest in computers and the desire to learn more about them. At the time the department (a customer service provider) made no use of information technology at all. It seemed to me that there was actually great scope to computerise several aspects of its operation, so I suggested that he give the 'difficult' staff member responsibility for investigating how the department might make use of computers, including producing a report with full costings. Some weeks later he reported to me that the computer project was proceeding extremely well, and that the staff member with whom he had such problems was now co-operative and, he said, 'visibly happier' too.

So take each of your staff in turn. Ask them what they actually do, even if such tasks and responsibilities are not listed in their formal job description. Better still, ask them to keep a diary for a few days (or weeks if the job is highly variable). People often forget to mention aspects of the job which they take for granted but which are actually very important for you to know about. For example, you may find that two or more people are sharing a task which you had previously thought of as belonging to just one of them. You may find that people are undertaking a much more substantial role as understudy to a more senior member of staff than you had realised (or than the senior had been prepared to admit!). Some jobs will turn out to be much more – or less – substantial or demanding than you thought. You may also find that some people are interpreting their role more widely than you had realised: self-empowerment may already be alive and working in your team!

Then sit down with each member of your staff in turn to discuss what he or she is doing, should be doing, and would like to be doing. With goodwill and a positive approach you should be able to negotiate a list of key tasks which offer the member of staff job satisfaction and the opportunity for growth and development, and which – overall – provides you with the assurance that organisational goals will be efficiently met. Once you have a list of key

94

tasks for each person (including yourself), it is possible to use them to produce a list of objectives.

These objectives, too, need to be negotiated. Staff need to feel that they have personal responsibility for achieving them. Objectives which are merely imposed from above will never have the same power to motivate that negotiated objectives have. Staff will feel much less responsible for achieving objectives which they have played no part in setting. They will feel that it is essentially up to the person who has set them to see that they are met. But if people are closely and genuinely involved in negotiating and setting their own objectives they feel they have ownership of them, and therefore a strong sense that it is up to them to achieve them.

This is also true of group objectives. You may find that some objectives need to be the shared responsibility of several members of the team, perhaps including yourself. In such cases everyone involved needs to be part of the process of setting the objectives and checking progress towards them.

95

## Setting 'SMART' objectives

Good objectives are the means by which you and your staff can exercise control over performance and work outcomes. But how can you be sure that the objectives you negotiate with your staff *are* good? Moreover, how can you ensure that staff can assess their own progress and exercise their own control over the achievement of these objectives? The answer as really quite simple. Make sure all staff objectives are SMART.

SMART objectives are:

- Specific
- Measurable
- Achievable
- Relevant
- Timed.

## SPECIFIC

Objectives need to be specific to both the individual and the key task to which they relate. They need to state precisely what needs to be done or achieved, so that individuals can assess for themselves whether or not they have been achieved. Broad general statements such as 'improve customer satisfaction' are not objectives, they are aims. Aims are useful as a means of setting a general direction, but they are a much less productive basis on which to assess progress. Specific objectives such as 'reduce number of customer complaints received annually' allow people to self-assess whether or not (or to what extent) the objective has been achieved.

## MEASURABLE

96

Objectives which cannot simply be answered 'yes' or 'no' need to be measurable in some way. An obvious example is an objective which includes a financial target, such as 'sell £500,000 worth of stock'. It is easy for the individual or group who own this objective to assess whether it has been fully realised or, if not, how far short performance has fallen. Other easily measurable objectives are those which express progress in percentage terms, for example 'reduce number of customer complaints received this year to 10 per cent less than last year'. Again, it is easy to self-check whether or not, or to what extent, this has been achieved.

## ACHIEVABLE

It's also essential to be sure that objectives really are achievable. Nothing is so demoralising to individuals or groups as objectives which are actually impossible. Nothing, that is, except objectives that are too easy to be worth striving for. This is another reason to involve your staff in setting objectives. They may have a much more realistic idea of what can really be achieved than you do. Of course, they may be over-ambitious and overestimate their own capabilities. On the other hand, they may be too cautious and set their sights too low (especially if they still fear failure). Your task as manager, therefore, is to help people to set objectives which are just low enough to be possible, and just high enough to motivate staff to increase performance.

The process is a little like teaching children to swim. Stand too close and they'll never swim further than they think they can; stand too far away and they'll be scared even to try. Get it right, and children gradually become confident, independent swimmers who no longer need you there just to make them feel safe because they know they can cope on their own.

## RELEVANT

Objectives which are not relevant to the needs of the organisation or the individuals who must achieve them are both pointless and wasteful of effort and resources. Yet there can sometimes be conflicts of interest to resolve. As a manager, you are expected to ensure that the objectives you and your staff set are not only compatible with overall organisational goals and objectives but as closely aligned with these as you can contrive. In an ideal world, every single personal objective of every single person within an organisation would be of direct and close relevance to the explicit goals of the organisation. But people also have personal agendas, and it is essential to recognise these too.

This is another reason for negotiating objectives with the individuals and groups who will own them. You need to ensure that the right balance is achieved between personal and group aspirations and the needs of the organisation as a whole. Where these conflict, the individuals or group need to be helped to recognise this so that, wherever possible, a compromise can be achieved in which both the organisation and the individual or group benefit. Where this cannot be achieved, and where there is evidence of real friction, you need to help your staff to recognise that it is ultimately in their own best interests to align their personal goals with those of the organisation. If someone really cannot do this, the most realistic option is for them to leave.

97

Such situations, however, are rare. More often what is needed is a set of group or personal objectives which achieves a motivating and constructive balance between meeting the legitimate needs and aspirations of your staff and the needs and goals of the organisation or department. Negotiation is again the key.

## TIMED

The most constructive objectives are those which have timescales attached to them. 'Increase productivity by 15 per cent by the end of this financial year' is much more productive than 'increase productivity by 15 per cent'. A timescale not only offers a clearer goal to strive for, it also incorporates a built-in control mechanism. At the appropriate time a check can be conducted to see if the objective has in fact been met. It also allows progress to be measured along the way to see if the objective is likely to be met by the specified time.

Regular control checks are essential for all objectives, even those without a specific timescale. When you and your staff negotiate objectives you should also decide when, and by whom, checks need to be made. For important objectives you may also wish to discuss who will confirm that a check *has* been made, and when this will happen. Often the most appropriate person to do this is someone who has managerial responsibility for the issue or area of concern. Sometimes, however, peer-checking is all that is required, and may be more appropriate to an organisation attempting to empower staff. Think about the procedures adopted by nurses for checking drugs administration or theatre equipment counts. There is no need here for a 'manager' to check: the responsibility is shared by peers. And if the procedure is safe enough for administering potentially dangerous drugs or checking that patients don't have a swab left inside them after an operation, then it's probably safe enough for most other organisational purposes too. So set up some sort of timed control check system and, where necessary, a system to check on the checks. Then stress to your staff the need to make sure you all stick to whatever you have agreed.

In practice, the appraisal process itself is an important opportunity for such checks, so it's important that you do appraise staff regularly and frequently enough for this to be of value. The most common timescale for formal appraisal interviews is yearly, and in a stable situation that is probably often enough. However in times of upheaval, or a major change such as introducing empowerment, more frequent appraisal is better. Not only does this give you the chance to check that all is going well, but it also offers staff formal feedback rather more often at a time when they may need the reassurance this can give.

Remember, too, that informal appraisal is still an important part of the management function, even when more formal systems have been introduced. A formal appraisal interview, no matter how frequent, is never a substitute for making sure that staff know how you view their performance at all times, nor is it ever a substitute for being open at all times to feedback from staff to you. Be aware of the need for both of these in addition to the formal appraisal process.

Above all, don't lose sight of the fact that appraisal should be directed at helping staff to achieve their objectives in their key tasks, not chastising them if they have not. There is an important difference between checking progress so that corrective action can be taken if need be, and policing behaviour. The checking aspect of appraisal should, just like the identification of key tasks and the setting of objectives, be a joint process. Staff should never fear that appraisal will uncover hitherto undisclosed failure, neither should any part of the process produce results which are a surprise to them.

If you have managed the initial negotiations about tasks and objectives well, and established proper, timed, self-checking systems, then staff will feel sufficient ownership of those tasks and objectives to be an equal partner in the appraisal process. Then you can work together to assess progress and negotiate about any changes, including revising unrealistic objectives, which may be needed or corrective action which may need to be taken.

But no matter who is responsible for checking that checks are made, and however and whenever it happens, it's essential that it *does* happen. Objectives which are never checked are no objectives at all. And objectives which have no timetable for checking are rarely checked. It is therefore essential to ensure that every single objective will be checked by someone – and sometimes by more than one person – at a specified time or times.

## SHARED CONTROL

In any organisation attempting to empower staff, then, a good appraisal system, backed up by clear, negotiated key tasks and SMART objectives, is essential. Setting direction and exercising control in an empowered organisation are essentially a matter of locating accountability further down the organisation, and of negotiating and sharing responsibility for control over outcomes. In empowered organisations control must become a team-based function and gaining staff commitment to both the principle and the process of shared control is fundamental to the success of empowerment.

# 7

# Breaking the barriers

So far, we have discussed worries about empowerment from the manager's point of view. We've looked at concerns about control and authority and seen how worries about these needn't be a barrier to empowering organisations. In doing so, empowerment has been treated as such a self-evidently 'Good Thing' that your staff could only greet the idea with open arms and keen enthusiasm. Well, your staff may indeed react like this. On the other hand, they might not.

In fact, staff, too, are often very sceptical of the whole idea when it is first presented to them, and may become downright resistant in the face of its implementation. Yet why should this be? We've seen how empowerment can release their abilities and offer them opportunities for self-development and a more satisfying working life. Why would anyone want to reject the idea of empowerment and resist its implementation?

## Reasons for resistance

Well, staff might resist empowerment for a number of reasons, some more straightforward than others. At its simplest, some of your staff have reservations for exactly the same reason you do: fear of loss of power. Staff with junior managerial or supervisory functions may feel particularly threatened by the fear that they will lose power and control as part of the empowerment process. They need to be offered the same reassurance that you were offered in chapter 1. You need to talk to them about these issues until they are satisfied that empowerment simply offers them a more effective way to achieve their aims.

But such staff may also have another level of concern: loss of status. As the rhyme says, 'a flea hath smaller fleas . . . and so . . . *ad infinitum*'. If power is to be devolved to everyone, where does that leave them in the flea-biting order? They may also fear that with loss of status will go loss of opportunity for promotion or career advancement. This fear may be particularly strong if your organisation has been involved in the kind of de-layering exercise which so many companies have recently undertaken. In such circumstances junior managers' and supervisors' fears should be treated particularly seriously. You will need their wholehearted support if empowerment is to be implemented effectively.

102

They need to be helped to understand that empowerment doesn't lead to fewer managers, but to less management. That is to say that managers remain as important as ever, but their role and function change from being predominantly leadership and con-trol, to facilitation and support. Talk to them about their fears and take their reservations seriously. Take them into your confidence about your own anxieties and concerns. Consider whether they will need some formal training to help them to adjust to their new role. Above all, help them to see not only the organisational benefits of empowerment and the reasons why you want to intro-duce it, but also the opportunities it will offer them to extend their management skills and experience.

Yet some staff without a formal supervisory or management role may also fear loss of power. In many organisations long-serving and senior staff may wield a substantial amount of informal power. They, too, may fear its loss, and the informal status that goes with it. What's more, such staff are often important opinion-formers within the organisation or department and may be able to exert substantial negative influence. These opinion-formers may not simply be individuals, but influential and powerful groups, often with a power base in some specific activity or skill. It's essential, therefore, that you identify such individuals and groups as early as possible. You need to be able to win their support if empowerment is to succeed. So it's worth taking some time to identify these influential individuals and groups. You need to know clearly who they are so that you can ensure that you win them over to your point of view. The entire empowerment process may depend on whether or not you can win – and keep – their support.

Who are the opinion-formers in your organisation? Of these, who is likely to support the idea of empowerment? They will be your key allies so identify them as early as you can. Then tell them what you plan so as to be sure of their support. Involve them in your planning and listen to their advice. They may have some very helpful views on how to avoid resistance and ensure acceptance. You also need to identify any opinion-formers who are likely to be doubtful about empowerment or even resistant to the idea. Could you convince them or change their views if need be? Who could help you to do this? The answer to the latter question may well be those opinion-formers who *do* support the idea. Use them to help you work on the doubters and the dissenters. If you can reach a certain critical mass of support you may find that much of the remaining resistance fades away. Where it does not, critics of the proposals are likely to find themselves isolated and without the necessary power base from which to mount a serious challenge to your plans. They may continue to criticise but are unlikely to be a real threat to the empowerment process.

103

However, there may also be a much more widespread problem affecting many or even all of your staff: simple fear of responsibility. You don't have to be an unreconstructed Theory X manager to recognise that in many organisations substantial numbers of staff *are* reluctant to accept any more responsibility than they feel they absolutely must, and avoid it whenever they can. Indeed the phenomenon is so common that we seldom pause to ask ourselves why this should be. Yet we know that when staff *are* persuaded to accept more responsibility they almost always rise to the challenge and, what's more, enjoy it too. So it's worth thinking about why people should so often choose to avoid rather than seek out opportunities for further responsibility.

The answer to the conundrum lies not in responsibility but in risk. When they look at the possibility of taking on more responsibility, many people also calculate what the consequences of taking on that responsibility might be. What they see is that risk is an unavoidable result of any responsibility. So when people reject the opportunity to take on more responsibility, what they are actually turning down is not responsibility but risk. Look further and it becomes clear that the risk they particularly wish to avoid is the risk of failure. If you never accept responsibility, they argue to themselves, you can never be blamed if things go wrong. So it's not responsibility itself that people are reluctant to accept, but responsibility for failure.

104

# Risk

The importance of tolerating well-intentioned errors has been repeatedly stressed. If you want your staff to accept more responsibility you have to reduce their fear of failure. But you also need to try to raise the level of their subjective assessment of the probability of success. Staff need to feel confident that they *will* be able to cope with increased responsibility, and that they will actually experience success, not failure. Often, however, the only way to persuade people that this is so is for them to experience it. Nothing succeeds like success, as the saying goes, and nothing so encourages further risk-taking than success at the early stages. What's more, observed success – watching others try and succeed at what we ourselves were nervous about attempting – can also be a powerful way of helping people overcome any initial anxieties.

The truth of this is graphically demonstrated on any adventure training course for managers. No one ever wants to be the first to jump. But once people see that others have taken the risk and succeeded their own nervousness recedes. So it is very important that people experience and observe success early in the empowerment process. We will return to this point. But before you can even begin you need to help people to deal with fear of risk you may have to overcome some of the other psychological barriers which are restraining them.

# Psychological barriers

There are a number of psychological barriers which you and your staff may have to overcome before you can successfully introduce empowerment to your organisation or department. You are likely to have to challenge and change people's attitudes, beliefs and expectations. You may even have to change some of your own. Of these, changing people's attitudes to the very idea of empowerment is the most important.

105

## CHANGING ATTITUDES

The most basic question which we all ask ourselves when faced with a possible change in the way we work is 'What's in it for me?' And if the answer is 'nothing at all', then we are unlikely to want to give the idea our full support. If the probable outcome, so far as we can see, will to be neutral for us personally, then we are likely to respond neutrally to the idea. If, however, we can foresee only negative outcomes (or if we believe that the overall impact will be negative) for us personally, our response is likely to be negative or downright hostile. Only if we can see the possibility of real and substantial personal benefit are we likely to greet new ideas and plans for change warmly and enthusiastically.

It is therefore of paramount importance that you help staff to identify *personal* benefits which empowerment might offer them. It's no good stressing, as so many change-management programmes do, the benefits to the organisation. Frankly that's not what concerns most people (unless they feel that their jobs are actually under threat). Appealing to people to accept change because it will help the organisation, team or department simply isn't enough. You need to persuade people that they will see some personal benefit too. And that benefit has to seem worth whatever investment of time, energy and mental effort you are asking them to make. It's no good offering people something *you* would regard as a benefit: it has to appeal to your staff, not you. You might regard better upward communication as a real personal benefit, and so it might be – for you. But it's unlikely to be the kind of thing which will light the fire of many of your staff.

So what does motivate people? Well, what motivates you? Money? Possibly, but financial incentives need to be fairly substantial to appeal to most people, assuming that their basic pay level is broadly satisfactory. People might be persuaded to put quite a lot of effort into something which would reliably pay an extra £200 every month, but few organisational changes offer that level of incentive. If the only foreseeable benefit is a few pounds more a month, then any effort required to achieve this would need to be quite small or else most people simply wouldn't think it worth the effort.

People are actually much more motivated by less tangible things such as personal development opportunities, doing something interesting and worthwhile, and even success itself. If staff can be helped to see that empowerment might offer them the chance to develop new skills and knowledge (especially if these are marketable) they might be keener on the idea. If you can also persuade them that it offers the opportunity to be involved in something genuinely beneficial and rewarding their interest may grow still further. And if you then stress the sheer buzz of being part of a successful initiative (to say nothing of the status which accrues to those who are involved in such a prominent project) then these may be all you need to persuade them to give it a try.

## CHANGING EXPECTATIONS

Of course, people also need to feel confident that there is a realistic possibility of them receiving whatever particular benefit they desire too. It's no good asking people to put a lot of effort into something if they feel that the chances of seeing the fruits of their labour are small. They simply won't bother to try. You need to be able to convince your staff that the changes you propose and the efforts and changes in working practice that you are asking them to make will actually bring them the benefits they seek. This is yet another reason why early success is essential. If people are prepared to give empowerment and you the benefit of the doubt they must be able to see real benefits early on in the process. If they can't see early success and real personal benefit from the start, they are unlikely to be willing to pay more than lip service to the idea of empowerment from then on. That's why careful planning (discussed in a later chapter) is essential to ensure that the empowerment process gets off to a flying start.

## CHANGING BELIEFS

You may also need to change some deeply ingrained beliefs about the nature of organisations and management. Such beliefs are likely to include the idea that it's management's job to manage, and theirs to do as they're told (whilst retaining the right to criticise management!). The notion that staff and managers might actually share responsibility for the success of the enterprise as equal partners may seem anything from odd to downright bizarre. Yet unless you can bring staff to accept this idea empowerment is doomed to fail.

# Magic helpers

One reason why staff may be reluctant to accept the idea of joint responsibilities lies in many people's deep-seated desire for what psychologist Eric Fromm calls 'Magic Helpers'. Magic Helpers are people on whom we feel we can rely to take care of us and tell us what to do. We choose to assume that they know more than we do and are therefore better placed to know what we ought to do. We want to be able to count on them to take decisions for us so that we don't have to grapple with the issues for ourselves. And – best of all – because Magic Helpers take the responsibility they also take the blame if it all goes wrong.

Some people are particularly prone to looking for Magic Helpers in their lives. These people tend to make extensive use of social and other agencies such as local church leaders, doctors, social workers and the like to advise them. Similarly, some people are particularly keen to be seen as Magic Helpers. Occupations particularly likely to attract them include teaching, medicine, social work – and management. It can be a very seductive role. It's quite an ego-booster to feel that someone relies on us to advise them and even tell them what to do. But it may not always be an appropriate one or even, ultimately, a truly helpful one. Of course, not all teachers, doctors, social workers or managers actual relish such a role. Many of them actively seek to reject it. Yet so strong is some people's need for one or more Magic Helpers in their life that they exert such substantial pressure on those they have chosen to occupy this role that rejecting it can be made very difficult.

108

But the need for a Magic Helper is not a fully adult response. It is essentially an immature one in anyone past adolescence. It is a refusal to accept full adult responsibility for oneself. Similarly, agreeing to play the role of Magic Helper to another adult is to deny the reality of an adult-to-adult relationship and substitute one of parent-to-child: hardly an appropriate relationship between managers and staff. The essential reason for empowerment is that it permits organisations to tap the full personal resources of all their staff. This is unlikely to happen if the relationship between managers and staff is based on the former treating the latter like children. True empowerment can only happen when all members of an organisation are treated – and behave – as fully-competent adults. Magic Helpers have no role to play in the empowered organisation.

But there is a dual problem here. Staff may exert considerable pressure on managers to continue to play the role of Magic Helper, not least because without such a helper they may be forced to look more closely at themselves when problems crop up. For many staff the great advantage of resisting empowerment is that they can retain the role of blameless critic when things go wrong. Moaning about the management is such an entrenched part of organisational life in many places that there can be considerable resistance to the idea of giving it up. If giving it up also means confronting one's own share of the responsibility for errors and problems then that resistance is compounded. Such people may prefer to remain in the relatively safe cocoon of childish dependence on others.

On the other side of the coin, managers may enjoy both the ego-trip and the power which accepting the role of Magic Helper confers. It can be very flattering to feel that organisational success depends on you, and that people rely on you for advice. On a more negative note, some people also get a real buzz from exercising power and control over others. One concomitant of this is that they may come to despise those over whom they exercise this power and who are under their control, and to doubt their capacity for self-management or even independent thought. Asking such people to relinquish both power and control is to ask them to give up much of what most motivates them as managers.

This is hardly a healthy state of affairs for any organisation, or for the individuals who work there. Yet, as we have seen, both sides of the Magic Helper relationship may be reluctant to give it up. Both will need to be convinced that any loss they may experience will be more than compensated for by the gains they will receive. Staff need to be persuaded that making full use of their knowledge and talents will offer them a more satisfying working life, and that the risks of self-determination and self-management are very small compared to the potential rewards. Managers need to be helped to see that the satisfaction to be gained from being a mentor is deeper and more extensive than that which can be achieved as a Magic Helper. They need to learn to accept that staff can be self-determining. They need to be helped to realise that they can actually extend their personal sphere of influence by reducing the exercise of power and control, and that, in doing so, their real impact on the progress of staff and the success of the organisation is increased. Only then will each side relinquish these familiar but ultimately sterile and destructive roles.

Yet, even if that problem is ironed out, a further – related – belief may need to be addressed and changed. Given that so many people wish to avoid responsibility, it may seem to them that the empowering manager is simply trying to slough off managerial responsibility on to others. In other words, your attempt to empower others may be misread as a simple refusal to accept the risks and responsibilities of the Magic Helper role – and people can become very angry when those they have unilaterally appointed to be their Helpers refuse to help. What you must do is help people to see that you are not divesting yourself of the problems of power but trying to share the benefits. The answer, as before, is to convince people that there are real potential benefits for them too in sharing power. This means being open about your motives and being prepared to share your hopes as well as your fears. Once people become convinced of your sincerity they are more likely to be willing to consider changing their own views.

## Overcoming resistance

What all this boils down to is that people won't necessarily *want* to be empowered at first. They may need persuasion. They may even need more than persuasion. You may actually feel that you need to use the positional power inherent in your managerial role to *force* people to accept power. This is the ultimate paradox: using power to devolve power may be the only way to achieve your aims. Yet if you simply try to force change through you are undermining the message you are trying to send, and indeed the entire process.

One solution to this apparent paradox is to start by relinquishing power gradually, rather than by insisting that others accept it, and to concentrate your attention on rewarding self-determination whenever it occurs. There will almost certainly be numerous occasions when you could simply desist from diving in and directing people, leaving them to cope for themselves instead. Teach yourself to resist helping unless it is absolutely essential, and avoid taking control just because others expect you to. Make it clear that you have every confidence in their ability to cope with the matter without help from anyone. Better still, try suggesting that they seek help from a colleague. If staff are to become empowered they will need to learn to recognise colleagues' skills and strengths as well as their own.

Similarly, you should take every opportunity to praise or otherwise reward initiative and self-direction in your staff. Make it plain that you welcome ideas and attempts to solve problems, even if they don't always quite work in practice. Once staff begin to realise that taking their own decisions is not only safe but praiseworthy, they are likely to take the risk more and more often.

111

With reasonable luck you will find at least one or two of your staff will actually welcome this new development. Encourage them all you can, and let other see that you are encouraging them. Eventually the message will begin to seep through to the rest of your staff that self-determination and initiative are what earns praise. If they also see that any well-intentioned errors are tolerated, and that failure is accepted as an opportunity for learning, then they may gradually be encouraged to make some more decisions for themselves.

By proceeding one step at a time in this way it is possible gradually to accustom people to rely on you a little less and on themselves and one another a little more, until you and they have actually moved a substantial part of the way towards empowerment without the word so much as being mentioned. Once you have prepared the ground in this way the idea is likely to be less of a surprise and seem less of a threat. You will also have built up a history of small successes you can point to, and staff who have enjoyed those successes will be supportive advocates for the proposed changes.

There are also five simple rules which will help you to overcome resistance to empowerment:

## SUPPORT INITIATIVE

If staff want to exercise initiative give them all the help and encouragement you can. If it goes wrong, continue to praise them for having tried, but also help them to learn from the experience so that failures can be avoided in future.

## FOSTER CREATIVITY

Encourage staff to look at situations and problems through fresh eyes and to try new approaches. One of the main reasons for empowerment, after all, is to harness fresh insights and ideas. So don't reject unfamiliar ideas or unusual answers.

## IMPROVE COMMUNICATION

Set up communication structures and systems which maximise the flow of information throughout the organisation or department: up, down, across, between – and any other direction you can think of! Make sure that people know that these structures and systems exist, and how to use them.

## REWARD EMPOWERED BEHAVIOUR

Once staff *do* begin to behave in ways which show that they have understood what empowerment is all about, reward them. Praise every single attempt to exercise personal or group initiative, even if it hasn't quite worked. Where one has worked, say so. Consider including empowered behaviour in your promotional and staff development criteria – and make sure everyone knows about it.

## WALK THE TALK

Finally, walk the talk – always. Model the behaviour you want to encourage. Don't just tell staff what empowered behaviour looks like: show them. And make sure that you don't slide back into old habits when the going gets tough or when your confidence falters.

# 8

# Staff development and reward systems

**A**ny major organisational change has implications for staff development, training and reward systems. This is particularly true of cultural changes such as empowerment.

## Training for empowerment

It is unlikely that all your staff already possess the full range of skills, attitudes and knowledge they – and you – will need if they are to get full benefit from, and make full contribution to, the process of empowerment. Staff will probably need to develop new skills in such areas as planning, problem identification and solving, teamwork, etc. But although it is easy to make such general predictions, more detailed identification of specific needs is essential if your staff are to be fully equipped for empowerment. You need to undertake a proper training needs analysis.

### TRAINING NEEDS ANALYSES

No matter what the size or nature of your organisation, and no matter what the level of background of your staff, a good training needs analysis (TNA) will always be based on the classic training-cycle model:

- identify performance shortfall (current or potential)
- identify ways in which training might rectify this
- implement appropriate training
- evaluate results
- repeat process, continuously.

Of these the first is, perhaps, the most important.

## Performance analysis

It is pointless to train people to acquire skills or knowledge which they already have, or which they don't actually need. It wastes time, money and effort, and is very demoralising. So the first essential in any training process is to identify real need.

There are various ways in which this can be done. One approach consists of manager-centred methods such as:

- observation
- tests and samples
- analysis of records

and each of these has its relative strengths and weaknesses.

## Observation

The most direct and perhaps the simplest approach is observation. Just watching people in the relevant range of situations can reveal performance shortfalls. However, many people feel threatened by being observed while they work. They may become so nervous that they make errors which they would not normally make. And even if this doesn't happen, it can be hard to observe what people know, as opposed to what they do. Furthermore, if the job is varied and complex, watching someone perform the full range of usual activities can be very time consuming indeed. It is therefore a method best suited to assessing practical performance of short and simple tasks.

115

## Tests and samples

Another direct approach is to ask people to complete tests or to take samples of their work. These are both effective techniques where the skills being examined are fairly simple and essentially practical in nature. Neither, however, is quite as simple as it might seem. It is difficult to ensure that any sample is truly representative of normal work, especially if acceptable standards for the task are fairly wide. It may be necessary to take a number of samples under a range of conditions for such samples to be really useful. Failure to do this can produce misleading results. Tests, too, may not always be as representative of the skills being examined as one might hope. Not only is nervousness a factor, but the test itself may be flawed or poorly assessed. Both methods share the weakness that their objectivity may be more apparent than real, and people may be misled into placing more reliance on the results than is really merited. This can be especially true of psychometric testing. These can be very useful and accurate when applied appropriately by a skilled practitioner. However not all such test are so used. In untrained hands, a badly-selected and badly-conducted test can be seriously misleading. You should be cautious about any such test unless it is conducted by a fully-accredited chartered psychologist.

116

## Analysis of records

Examining existing records is often overlooked as a source of information about training needs yet it can be a very simple and effective approach. Records which may be of particular value when undertaking a TNA are customer complaints or comments, records of faults and errors, minutes of meetings, accident report books and, of course, staff appraisal forms. The approach does, however, rely on records being accurate, up to date and in a suitable form for analysis for training purposes. It can also be difficult to know which records are likely to be of value and access to some may be restricted. Furthermore, it may be difficult to identify particular records with specific individuals or even groups. Most such sources (with the exception of appraisal forms) are probably most suitable for getting a broad, general picture of training needs.

## STAFF-CENTRED APPROACHES

None of the preceding approaches allows much direct involvement of the staff whose needs you are assessing. They may not, therefore, be the best methods to use in an organisation which is attempting to empower staff. It has already been stressed that managers need to 'walk the talk' if staff are to be convinced that empowerment is real and important. This also applies to the choice of management systems and methods: they, too, need to reflect the values and practices of empowerment. If you seriously intend to empower staff, then you need to choose a TNA method which empowers them too, and which allows them to play a full part in the assessment process.

117

Approaches which involve staff more directly, include questionnaires and interviews. Each of these also has its own strengths and weaknesses, and each is more suited to some circumstances than others.

### Questionnaires

If you need to assess the training needs of large numbers of people *and* you can rely on self-assessment, then questionnaires can be useful. But they seldom result in a full response. A return rate of around 60 per cent or so is typical, so they may not produce all the information you need. What's more, good questionnaires are *much* harder to construct than people realise.

I have never seen anyone who lacks formal training in questionnaire design produce an adequate one, let alone a good one. Even people who believe they have ample experience in producing them frequently make basic, but serious, errors. The trouble is that, without formal training, people seldom realise that they are making errors. Even the simplest of questionnaires may contain a number of them. That's why my advice to managers who want to use questionnaires is always the same: don't! Don't, that is, unless you are willing to read up on the subject thoroughly and take the lengthy process – design, pilot, re-design, re-pilot, and only then, finally, use – seriously.

Even then there can be problems. Even if the questionnaire 'works' as a device, it may not tell you what you need to know. The golden rule of questionnaire design is: never ask a question unless you know exactly why you want that information *and* exactly what you're going to do with it once you've got it. It's amazing how far people can get into the process of questionnaire design without realising the importance of this rule. I once received a frantic telephone call from the manager of a service organisation which had spent weeks surveying its customers. Response had been good, with the result that they had more than 5,000 returned forms to process. It was only when they counted them that they realised that they had no idea how to process or analyse the replies. I agreed to look at them to see if anything could be done. Not a chance! They were they too badly designed. Questions were ambiguous, producing confusing replies and in several places there were overlapping categories making accurate analysis impossible. Worse, it was quite clear that whoever had written the questionnaires really had no clear idea what information was needed, or why. The writer seemed simply to have asked as many questions as he or she could dream up about absolutely anything and everything. Now, even quite a short questionnaire takes considerable time and effort to analyse. A longer one really needs to be computer-analysed and designed especially for that purpose. This one was several pages long and its writer clearly hadn't given a moment's thought to how it was to be analysed. It was a disaster. The only thing I could do was advise them to ditch it and start again.

I suspect, however, that they found a less scrupulous consultant who helped them to commit the third and final error of questionnaires: taking the results of bad questionnaires seriously. There is an acronym in computing: GIGO ('garbage in, garbage out'). The same applies to questionnaires. The trouble is, the results can look very impressive: all those rows of figures and percentages and the pretty charts. It all looks so precise and detailed that it's easy to forget that the results are only as sound as the questions asked – and, unless it was constructed by an expert, the chances are that they were flawed. And, of course, once you have gone to all the trouble of printing, distributing, collecting and analysing them it's hard to accept that the whole exercise has been pointless.

So approach the use of questionnaires with care, and some trepidation. Regard them as a last, rather than first, resort unless you can afford to employ an expert to help you design and process them. Of course, if yours is a large organisation and you need to analyse the training needs of a large number of staff it may well be worth the time and expense of doing this since most of the alternative approaches would actually be too time consuming. A good questionnaire may actually be the best approach in such circumstances (providing that it *is* a good one, that is).

119

## Interviews

Interviews can be a very effective way to glean information about training needs. In a large organisation you may be able to interview only a sample of the staff, drawn from the groups or levels whose training needs you are interested in discovering. In these circumstances they can help you form a broad picture of the general pattern of needs. Try to interview not just representatives of the group whose training needs you are researching, but some, at least, of their supervisors or managers too. They may be aware of needs that individuals are unable (or unwilling) to identify for themselves.

In a smaller organisation or department you may be able to conduct individual interviews with each person whose needs you are trying to identify. This allows you to tailor your proposed solutions very closely to individuals and their specific needs. But, again, individual members of staff may not be fully aware of or open about their own needs so unless you are their direct line manager you need to interview whoever most closely supervises their work too, to get a fully-rounded picture.

You also need to give some thought to whether the interview should be structured, unstructured or somewhere in between. Structured formats ensure that you cover all the main issues and points and make it easy to collate information from a series of interviews to produce a picture of the aggregated needs of the team or department. On the other hand, they may be too narrow and rigid to uncover unexpected or unusual needs. Unstructured formats allow you to explore individual needs freely and in depth, but may be difficult and time consuming to analyse. You also need to think about whether or not you will tape-record the interviews, or record the results in writing at the time. As a rule of thumb, there is little point in taping highly-structured interviews since the answers are likely to be predictable and easy to record. Unstructured interviews are probably better if you tape them. Not only does this ensure that you are able to capture all the interviewee's responses, but knowing that it is all being recorded can free you to concentrate on conducting the interview. Unstructured interviews require more skill. You need to be able to manage the process so that the interviewee feels relaxed and able to respond freely, whilst still ensuring that the main issues are thoroughly explored.

120

Another variation to consider is whether you should interview people singly or in groups. People may feel able to be more open and self-disclosing in individual interviews, but group interviews can help to spark ideas and insights which individuals might not have produced, and make it easier to see where consensus about group training needs lies. Group interviews, too, need a skilled facilitator if they are to be productive but, if run well, can be a very suitable and effective way to empower staff to contribute to the analysis of training needs.

The commonest kind of TNA interview is, of course, the appraisal interview. If your organisation has a good, regular appraisal system, the analysis of training needs during such interviews will be part of your normal practice. You will also be constrained to some extent by your organisation's appraisal scheme in terms of the kind of interviews you can conduct. If your organisation has no appraisal scheme of any kind you might wish to explore the possibility of establishing one, if only in your own team or department. But even a good appraisal scheme may be geared towards the identification of individual needs, rather than those of groups of staff. You might, therefore, wish to consider conducting regular group interviews in addition to individual appraisals to try to identify common interests and needs.

It is impossible to anticipate here the precise training that a comprehensive TNA of your staff will uncover. It is, however, possible to suggest some specific problem-solving techniques which almost all staff entering an empowerment programme are likely to find helpful, and which will need to be introduced through formal training. Details of these will be found in chapter 9, together with suggestions as to how they might be introduced.

121

## Organisational goals

One further factor must be stressed. It is essential that all TNAs retain a tight focus on organisational visions, goals and objectives. Training should not be a reward or an extravagant gesture. It is a substantial organisational investment and needs to be planned and monitored as carefully as any other investment would be. Like any other investment, too, it needs to be closely linked to organisational objectives if it is not to be pointlessly squandered. So whatever method is chosen to explore training needs you need to keep these organisational goals firmly in mind in order to ensure that individual aspirations are in alignment with organisational needs.

Yet, if you are truly committed to empowerment you should try to avoid being unduly instrumental about the kinds of training which you are prepared to support. You may find that staff express a desire for training which does not seem to be directly related to their immediate post or even to their next possible appointment. Before you reject the idea, though, you should consider whether by meeting the request for this training you will retain a member of staff you would prefer not to lose, or – just as importantly – retain his or her motivation and enthusiasm for the job and organisation. It may be possible to offer partial support for training which is likely to be of real value to a particular individual or group even though its direct relevance to organisational goals is less clear.

# Funding training

There is no point whatever in conducting an analysis of training needs if you have neither the means nor the intention of paying for it. Without a budget the exercise is pointless. The only exception to this is where you intend to use the results of the analysis to persuade senior management that such a budget is needed. Any organisation or department which fails to identify a specific budget for training its staff is neglecting its human resources and failing to capitalise fully on one of its most valuable assets. One way to decide on the budget is to set it as a percentage of turnover or salaries. For the price of a tiny percentage of income or staff costs enlightened organisations can reap high benefits. Government researchers have shown that these organisations are more able to ride out a recession than those which do not invest in training, which makes it all the more regrettable that training is where some organisations look first – instead of last – to make savings. Never was an economy more false or misguided.

So if your TNA has revealed genuine training needs it is important to fund them properly. Of course it may not be realistic to attempt to meet all needs immediately, and common sense makes it plain that not all needs will be equally urgent or important. So it's necessary to try to set some priorities so that you can be sure that training funds are invested where they are most needed and most urgent. One way to do this is by a simple points system. You can take each identified need and allocate it a number of points depending on its:

- urgency
- congruence with organisational objectives
- seriousness
- importance to the individual
- importance to the group
- cost versus probable benefit

or whatever other factors are important in your circumstances, such as time needed away from the job, etc. Once you have allocated points in this way it is relatively easy to set priorities. It might be a good idea to involve your staff in this process. It's much easier to accept that your application for funding for a training course has been turned down if you are aware of the process by which this happened and the criteria on which the decision was made.

123

One further factor which it is important not to overlook is the number of times a particular need has previously been identified or training requested. There is a danger that a priority system which does not take these into account may continue to ignore the needs of a particular individual or group time after time because the particular need or request never quite scores sufficiently in the priority stakes to get funding. Yet it can be very demoralising to have one's need or request rejected over and over again. If you include an assessment of the length of time a need has existed in your priority scoring system you will avoid this common morale-sapping error.

Other ways exist for you to fund the low-priority training needs of particular individuals or groups. Where these needs relate as much to personal development as to organisational needs part-funding may be the answer. Staff may be happy to contribute financially to their own training where they can see some personal benefit, as well as benefit to the organisation. The exact proportion of personal and organisational funds will need to be negotiated but should be based on an assessment of the proportional benefit likely to be derived from the training by each. A further option is the loan of training fees, to be repaid out of salary over a comfortable period and either interest-free or at a low rate. You may also be able to provide references or guarantees for training loans from other sources. Most high street banks now operate such schemes.

## NON-FINANCIAL SUPPORT

Funding, however, is not the only support which you can offer staff: time and encouragement are equally important. Even if you can't find the cash for direct financial support for training you may be able to provide time instead. This might be meeting time to allow groups or pairs of staff to share skills, knowledge and ideas. You may be able to offer time off to attend a free course, or one which individuals have funded (or part-funded) themselves; or offer study-leave for exams. Where there is likely to be any benefit at all to the organisation, this time should be treated as paid leave. Only as a last resort should you ask staff to take unpaid leave for training which has organisational benefits of any kind, and asking staff (as some organisations do) to use their own holiday entitlement for such purposes sends a clear message that you have no interest in that individual's endeavours to increase his or her skills and knowledge: few things are as demoralising as this. Such a response has no place in any organisation which is serious about its staff or about empowerment.

Lastly, simple interest and encouragement are just as important as other kinds of support. Talk to your staff about what they are learning and make sure that success is noticed. Better still, find ways to enable staff to pass on what they have learned from their training to others. Run skills-sharing sessions wherever you can. Ask staff who have attended courses or conferences to report back afterwards at meetings or in memos. Let everyone know when someone has passed an exam or received a qualification. When achievement has been substantial, celebrate! Buy the achiever a cake and a bottle of bubbly, and present it to them publicly. Place a photograph of the event in the company magazine or newsletter, or even the local newspaper. Let your customers and clients know. In other words, make every possible effort to ensure that everyone knows that you recognise that training matters and that you support it wholeheartedly.

# Transitional reward systems

You also need to pay attention to your organisation's reward systems. In an ideal world, the intrinsic rewards staff gain from working for a well-managed organisation should far outweigh any additional rewards bestowed by the management. In a fully empowered organisation staff would be fully motivated by an appropriate wage or salary and their own sense of a job done well. In a fully adult-to-adult working relationship staff would not depend for their sense of achievement on formal rewards conferred by their managers. They would generate this for themselves.

In the shorter term, however, it is more realistic to accept that formal reward systems operated by management can be an effective way to support the empowerment process. Any such reward system must explicitly support the aims of empowerment and stress its importance to both the organisation and the individual. If possible these systems should include financial rewards for successful empowered behaviour, and a pay and reward structure which recognises the additional skills and responsibilities which empowerment may require.

However, unless you are a very senior manager or part of a very small organisation, you may not have much direct influence on the overall pay and reward system of the organisation. Nonetheless, you may still have considerable scope for developing a reward system for your staff which supports empowerment and empowered behaviour. You may have sufficient discretion over your own budget to be able to devise a bonus system which rewards empowered action and attitudes. If so, the idea is worth considering. The value of such awards need not be high. The important thing is that they provide some kind of tangible recognition of effort and success. But bear in mind that the former is as important as the latter: you need to reward effort even if it does not result in immediate success if people are to feel encouraged to take sensible risks and try new ideas.

Small tokens are often a useful device too. They need not cost much but, if they are imaginative, can have a substantial impact on motivation and effort. A bunch of flowers (and not just for women: men like flowers too) and a card with an encouraging message can boost morale enormously, as can a bottle of decent wine or a gift which reflects the recipient's interests. None of these need cost very much but, as the saying goes, it's the thought that counts. That's why such personally-chosen rewards are so much more effective than any of mass-produced 'incentives'. And you can double the impact by presenting the reward publicly and prominently.

126

But you probably do have one major financial reward within your sphere of control, and that is promotion. You need to make sure that promotion and assessment criteria emphasise empowerment and empowered behaviour, and that staff know this. If they realise that their next career move may depend on the extent to which they are able to accept empowerment and empower others, they are likely to focus efforts in this direction. Such a simple policy can achieve substantial results.

## NON-FINANCIAL REWARDS

In addition to financial rewards and gifts you need to try to find some new forms of recognition of effort and achievement to reinforce empowered attitudes and behaviour. These can be elaborate or very simple, and sometimes the corniest ideas can have great impact. One management educator I know sometimes sticks gold stars on particularly good assignments, and finds that even his most sophisticated students respond with grins of sheepish delight. One of my own management research students tells me she always looks out for the smiley faces I sometimes draw as a comment on her work-in-progress, and feels quite disappointed if she doesn't find any!

Praise of any kind is an invaluable part of any reward system. You can give praise directly or by memo (with copies to other people so that the person being praised knows that others know about it too). You can also publish praise in company newsletters, and so on. But however it is delivered it is important that the recipient (and the audience, if there is one) value it. This means it must be sincere, and not mechanical, and it must not be in a coin which has become debased through over-use. Sadly, some managers seem to have taken the 'praise your staff' message too much to heart. They lavish praise from morning till night, and in all directions. The result is that no one (not even the manager) takes it seriously. The trick is to be sparing – but not stingy – with praise, and use it only when you really mean it. Staff will value it so much more.

127

## INTANGIBLE REWARDS

Empowerment itself offers a number of intangible rewards for managers and their staff. It is an important staff development strategy in its own right. Successful empowerment offers staff personal growth, skill enhancement, and the chance to develop transferable and marketable skills and experience. It's therefore important that you help your staff to recognise these too if they are to give wholehearted support to the empowerment process. Yet such intangible, intrinsic benefits may not always be as visible to your staff as they are to you. You may need to ensure that these benefits are repeatedly stressed in all discussions of empowerment.

It's also important to focus on these intangible rewards for another reason. It is inappropriate in an empowered organisation for all rewards to continue to remain in the hands of management. If this is the case true empowerment can hardly be said to have happened. Even praise can be a rather paternalistic tool. So stress that the most important rewards of empowerment are not yours to give. They are a direct result of the employees' own empowered behaviour.

## PEER AWARDS

There is one further important step you can take to encourage empowered behaviour in both management and staff: set up empowerment award groups. Such groups need to be staffed by volunteers from every level within the organisation, and given a budget over which they have complete control. Then they should be empowered to award bonuses or gifts to staff who have demonstrated particular effort or achievement in the context of empowerment. They can distribute such awards either on the basis of their own knowledge of who is doing what or by seeking nominations from others. You'll have to leave them to decide on the basis of local circumstances. Your role in this process should be minimal: negotiating a budget and, perhaps, nominating possible candidates for awards on the same basis as anyone else.

Devolving substantial and untrammelled power to endow awards to such a group sends a powerful message that managers are no longer the only people whose opinion counts, or whose approbation is worth seeking. If you are serious about empowering your staff you also need to empower them to decide who will be rewarded, and how.

# 9

# Systems, strategies and techniques

The will to empower is not enough. You need to take action to ensure that your staff are able to play the full role in the organisation's progress and development that empowerment promises. Staff need to have the support of appropriate systems, strategies and techniques if they, and you, are to be able to make full use of their skills and knowledge.

129

## Systems

The first essential in any attempt to empower staff is an efficient and comprehensive communication system or, more properly, systems. You need to ensure that communication channels are

- sufficient
- accessible
- multi-dimensional

if information is to flow as freely and directly as it should. Above all, it is essential that information should be able to flow *from* staff, as well as to them.

In most organisations the flow of information and ideas tends to be downwards. Although attempts sometimes emanate from the top of the organisation to seek a specific response or particular information from staff, it is less common for staff themselves to initiate upwards communication beyond their immediate line management. This is because, typically, few (if any) channels exist to allow staff to *instigate* an upward flow. Vertical communication usually consists of management telling or asking: team briefings, memos, company newsletters or magazines, questionnaires and so on. Only rarely, however, does the vertical flow of information in most organisations include a system designed specifically to support staff initiating the telling or doing the asking.

Yet if staff are to be fully empowered then it is essential that they should have easy access to channels of upward communication which are within their own control. Setting this up is sometimes as simple a matter as ensuring that staff know who, at senior management level, is responsible for what and where they can be found. Where concerns or queries seem likely to arise frequently then some more formal system such as a regular 'surgery', rather like those which MPs hold in their constituencies, at which staff can contact senior managers, may need to be set up. The precise circumstances of each organisation will dictate the number and nature of the systems necessary to ensure that information or enquiries flow as easily and rapidly upwards through the organisation as they do downwards.

One important lesson to be learned from Total Quality Management is that staff-initiated upwards communication of errors or problems is crucial to organisational success. Yet, as we saw in chapter 4, few organisations have an upwards-communication system in place. Any organisation aiming at staff empowerment, however, must make it a priority to ensure that such a system exists. Unless staff have easy access to a system which allows them to alert the organisation to problems and failures, no true empowerment is possible.

## ERROR IDENTIFICATION SYSTEMS

Setting up an error identification system need not be either complicated or difficult. In its simplest form all that is required is that every employee should have easy and reliable access to a supply of simple forms which allow them to notify the problem or error. The form should simply ask for the name of the notifier, where he or she works, the date, and a brief outline of the fault or problem. All forms should be sent to or collected regularly by a central co-ordinator (or group) who then accepts ownership for the problem, taking responsibility either for solving it (or putting the error right) personally, or for ensuring that someone else does so. This co-ordinator or group also needs to ensure that the person who originally notified the issue is kept informed of progress at all times until the matter is resolved. In the best systems a problem or error remains 'live' until the person who notified it is satisfied that it has been solved or put right and has indicated this by signing the form to say so. Only then can the co-ordinator regard the matter as closed.

131

Such a system is not only empowering for the individual who reports the problem, but is also of immense value in offering the staff who take ownership of the notified problem and try to resolve it opportunities for personal and even career development. Taking part in such a process makes good use of staff talents and abilities to improve organisational efficiency and effectiveness, and is highly motivating for all those involved. Being able to tackle problems and produce effective solutions can be very satisfying indeed. It is also an important vehicle for skill development and may offer both staff and their managers the opportunity to assess individual potential for future career development.

It's also important to keep careful and accurate records of all difficulties notified, so that it is possible to keep a check on how quickly any particular issue is resolved, and also to get a sense of how often similar problems are notified, or whether a number of related problems seem to crop up. It's essential to try to establish whether a pattern of any kind is discernible and, if so, what it is and where it might lie. Then appropriate action may be taken to tackle the root causes. Staff can be involved in such a process in two main ways: Error Correction Teams and Quality Circles.

# Strategies

Error Correction Teams (ECTs) bring together people with a wide range of skills and experience who take ownership of a problem until it is solved. Team members needn't all have specialist or technical knowledge of the problem issue. In fact there is some value in including a sprinkling of people who don't have such specialist skills as they can often offer a different, fruitful perspective from the experts', who may be too close to the problem to see a novel solution. Such teams are a speedy and practical way to tackle simple problems quickly. They are most effective if the members have received some formal training in Quality techniques or creative problem-solving methods so that they are able to use a range of conceptual and practical tools. A few of these techniques are discussed later in this chapter.

132

ECTs need not have a long lifespan. They may come together simply to solve one particular problem then disband, or they may have a semi-permanent existence. Ideally, though, all staff should have the opportunity to play a part in such a team, so it may be more productive deliberately to limit the teams' life so that everyone has a chance to be involved in one over a reasonably short time span. Another way to ensure that everyone gets the chance to be involved is to rotate membership of a permanent team on a regular basis. The size and nature of your organisation will dictate the best solution for your particular circumstances.

Quality Circles (QCs) are not as efficient or fast at solving problems as ECT but they can be a very effective way to bring underlying problems to the surface. They can be particularly useful in situations where you or your staff begin to suspect that a series of apparently unconnected minor problems may have a common cause. QCs also have a role to play where no particular problems have been identified but where staff wish to explore ways in which Quality and organisational efficiency might be improved. QCs typically take rather a long time to achieve their results (so use an ECT if you need speedy action) but they can be a very effective way to develop and involve staff as well as solve problems. For these reasons membership of a QC involves a long-term commitment from staff. Bear in mind, too, that both approaches are most effective when membership is drawn from different functional parts of the organisation. The trickiest problems are often those which arise in the interstices between departments rather than within just one. Horizontal communication is as important as vertical.

# Techniques

If staff are to play a full part in the work of the organisation or department they need to be given the tools which will enable them to do so. Ideally you and your staff should adopt a structured approach to organisational improvement. One such structure might be:

133

- problem finding
- problem analysis
- idea generation
- idea evaluation
- idea testing
- planning and monitoring implementation.

There exists a plethora of techniques appropriate to each part of this process. The next section suggests possible ways of approaching each of these stages in the problem-solving process, using one technique from the wide range available and explaining how you might use it.

## PROBLEM FINDING

The idea of trying to find problems to solve may seem odd. The notion that it's best not to prod slumbering dogs for fear that they should wake up and bite you is understandable. Few managers see the point in looking for trouble since they suspect that they're bound to find it if they do. Many managers hold strongly to such ideas, and have a marked reluctance to the notion that they should start a process of organisational change by trying to find problems, since they usually feel that they have quite enough to deal with as it is.

But remember that the whole point of empowerment is to free you to take a more strategic approach to management. What's more, you can't find what's not there. Just because you haven't yet spotted these problems doesn't mean they don't exist. You may have been so busy dodging the arrows of the army of problems that currently beset you that you haven't yet seen the new ones waiting on the horizon. So you're not prepared for them. If only you were able to lift your head high enough over the parapet to be able to see them you might be able to take pre-emptive action before they become a real threat.

There is a wide variety of techniques which might be used in a structured process, starting with problem finding and moving through to implementation. Examples of such techniques include:

- SWOT analysis (problem finding)
- Five Ws and an H (problem analysis)
- Brainstorming (idea generation)
- Dots and Spots (evaluation)
- Reverse Brainstorming (testing)
- Panic Buttons (planned implementation).

Each of these will now be explained in detail.


## SWOT analysis

SWOT analysis is a very simple problem-finding technique which helps groups to focus on the organisation or department. It consists of generating separate lists of an organisation's or department's

- Strengths
- Weaknesses
- Opportunities

- Threats

to try to form a clear picture of the problems you may be facing now or in the future, together with an inventory of the resources you have at your disposal to combat them.

All you need is a flipchart sheet divided vertically and laterally into four equal segments. Label the top left segment 'Strengths' and the top right one 'Weaknesses'; the bottom two segments should be labelled 'Opportunities' (left) and 'Threats'. Now simply ask people to try to list items for inclusion in each segment. It's important to try to be objective and realistic, avoiding either undue optimism or unnecessary pessimism. It's also a good idea to check the validity of each item you include by asking for *evidence* to support the assertion, or for an example which substantiates it. You might perhaps validate the assertion that you have a well-trained workforce by reminding people that the company recently won a National Training Award. Or you might offer as an example of your weaknesses in new product development the loss of a major client to a competitor with a new product range.

135

SWOT analysis offers an easy but useful framework (which virtually everyone can understand) for undertaking an analysis on which to build plans for future developments. You can use the technique to explore general aspects of the organisation and its environment, or you can use it to explore a particular set of circumstances. In the latter case you might, for example, undertake a SWOT analysis in terms of the changes to your business environment caused by new legislation or new technological developments. If you intend to do this then it is important that all the participants fully understand the nature and impact of the new legislation or technical developments, so you may need to run a short briefing session first.

Once you have begun to identify some possible problems you then need to look closely at them to ensure that you have fully grasped their nature, extent and possible impact. For that you need a problem analysis technique.

## Five Ws and an H

This is another very simple way to get groups examining problems. It consists of asking those five perennially useful 'W' questions: Who? What? Where? When? and Why? and that very important 'H' one: How? in order to explore the problem fully.

The best approach is to take each W in turn and generate as many questions based on it as you can. You might, for example, ask:

- Who does the problem affect?
- Who has solved a problem like this in the past?
- Who has the skills to solve this?
- Who should we tell about the problem?
- Who is acting as a block to solving it?

Similarly you might ask:

- What is the extent of the problem?
- What will happen if we don't solve it?
- What will happen if we do?
- What resources do we need to tackle it?
- What other information about the problem do we need?

Turning to the H you might list:

- How did the problem come about?
- How do we know?
- How can we tell if we've solved it?
- How important is it?
- How much time have we got to solve it?

In each case ask as many other relevant questions as you can think of.

Don't try to answer any of the questions at this stage: just generate as many as you can. You then take each group of questions in turn and try to answer them, one by one. Concentrate simply on answering the questions, not solving the problem itself. That comes later. Of course if any ideas do occur, keep a record of them. But the purpose of this technique is not to find solutions to the problem but answers to these questions, so that you have a much better grasp of the nature and extent of the problem when you do come to try to solve it.

This is not likely to be a short process so you need to allow plenty of time for this technique, perhaps over several meetings if the size or severity of the problem warrants it. You might want to tackle just one W at a single meeting. But however you manage the process, by the end you should have a much deeper and better understanding of the problem. Then you're ready to tackle the next stage: generating ideas.

## Brainstorming

One important idea-generation technique is brainstorming. Yet few problem-solving techniques can have been so misused and abused over the years. The term tends to be used loosely to cover virtually any situation in which a group of people make lists of any kind. No wonder that its real value is so often overlooked. Managed properly it is a powerful technique for generating ideas and solutions which might otherwise never surface. It is also an effective way to help a group begin to work together efficiently and harmoniously.

The only requirements for running a brainstorming session are a group of (ideally) between five and nine people, a group leader (and, ideally, a leader's assistant who can write quickly and legibly) a flipchart and pens, some means of displaying completed sheets so that all can see them, and a poster (or posters) prominently displaying the rules of brainstorming. (If you didn't know there were any rules you've almost certainly not been doing it properly!)

A good brainstorming session will last about twenty to thirty minutes (not more than about forty minutes at most), during which time a good group should be able to produce well over a hundred ideas. All of these ideas should be written verbatim on a flipchart and the completed sheets displayed so that all the ideas remain visible at all times. Before you begin, explain to the group that the purpose of brainstorming is to generate as many possible solutions for a given problem as possible. Write the problem as succinctly as possible on the first flipchart sheet, in the form: 'In what ways might . . .' For example, you might write: 'In what ways might we shorten the production cycle.?' or 'In what ways might waste be reduced?' Explain that the group is to call out any idea which occurs to them and that this will be written on the flipchart. Stress that no one is to question or criticise any idea (even in fun) and then outline the four rules of brainstorming: go for quantity; suspend judgement; freewheel; hitch-hike.

'Go for quantity' means that the aim is to generate as many ideas as possible without at this stage worrying whether they are 'good' (or even possible) solutions. That's why the second rule, 'suspend judgement', is important. Stress that people should not criticise any ideas, even their own, and should not self-censor either but shout out any idea no matter how silly or wild. Point out that in a good brainstorming session it is often the wildest ideas which turn out to contain the seed of a really useful and original solution. Generating a stream of ideas requires the ability to freewheel, or randomly associate so that's rule three. The final rule stresses the value of using ideas that have been called out to generate further ones by 'hitch-hiking', using one idea to stimulate another and carry it further forward. Finally, pin the rules up so that they remain visible throughout the session. Now you're ready to begin.

Every brainstorming session must start with a warm-up of some kind. A simple way to do this is to take any handy object such as a pen top or a teaspoon and ask the group to think of as many alternative uses for the object as they can. Ask the group to call out any idea which occurs to them, but don't write them down. The idea is to encourage the group to think creatively and uninhibitedly so don't criticise or mock any idea (or allow anyone else to do so either). In fact you should positively welcome crazy or off-beat suggestions, especially if they are funny. Laughter, in my experience, is a key factor in successful brainstorming sessions.

138

Allow the warm-up to run for three or four minutes (or until ideas begin to fail) then start the brainstorming session itself. Remind the group of the rules for brainstorming and read out the problem. Then let them begin. Ideas are typically plentiful at the beginning and it is important that these are recorded quickly so as not to interrupt the flow. It's equally important, though, to make sure that all are recorded so don't miss any out. Encourage the group to keep the ideas coming but don't worry if there are occasional pauses: the flow will usually start again within a few seconds. If it does not and you want to regenerate momentum, there are a number of things you can do: silent incubation; wild ideas; and excursions. Silent incubation means deliberately stopping the flow of ideas for a timed, one-minute interval during which the group should be asked to look carefully at the ideas they have already generated to see if they can hitch-hike from these to some new ones. At the end of the minute you can start them off again calling out ideas. Another approach which is useful if the ideas being generated lack sparkle or originality is to say that for the next five minutes you want people to concentrate on generating wild ideas: the wilder the better. A further way to lift the group out of a rut of banal solutions or to help them if they are running out of ideas is to ask them all to look out of the window. Choose an object – any object at all – that they can all see, and ask them to think for a few seconds about how that object might relate to or be considered a metaphor for the problem under consideration. Then ask them to start generating ideas using the object as a springboard.

139

If you are leading the group well there should be a sense of fun as well as serious intentions, and laughter is usually a sign that the group is thinking creatively and freely. Let the session run until you sense that there is no more value in continuing, using silent incubation, the wild idea instruction and excursions as necessary to help the group get over any 'stuck' periods.

At the end of the session the group should review the ideas, selecting those which seem to have potential for further exploration and development. If the session has worked well you should find that the group has generated such a plethora of ideas that you will need to apply another set of techniques to select the most promising ones and evaluate them.

## Dots and spots

One very simple way to identify those ideas from a brainstorming session which seem most likely to be worth further exploration is to give every member of the group either a set of coloured sticky dots (available from all office stationers) or a felt-tipped pen. Make sure that everyone has a different colour of dot or pen so that each individual's response can be identified. (In large groups you may need to use dots of different sizes to distinguish people too.)

Then just ask people to stick a dot (or use their pen to colour a spot) next to the ideas which seem to them to be the most important ones to consider further. Remind them not to reject apparently wild ideas as these may actually be the very ones which, after modification, offer the most radical and effective solutions. It's a good idea to ration the number of dots or spots that people can use or they will not be sufficiently selective. As a rule of thumb, you should limit the number of dots or spots people can award to no more than 10 per cent of the total number of ideas generated. Point out that people can award one or more dots or spots to any idea, up to their overall maximum. Stress that they shouldn't allow themselves to be influenced by anyone else: it's their own personal opinion that is wanted. Similarly, no lobbying is allowed. They mustn't question anyone else about their choice or criticise it, or try to influence other people's selections in any way. Allow up to about ten minutes for people to make their selections before bringing the group together again.

Now invite them to ask one another clarifying questions in order to discover the thinking behind any choice of idea which puzzles them. The point of this is not to criticise other people's choices or force them to justify them but merely to offer the opportunity to explore one another's thinking. It may be, for example, that the impact of one idea is not immediately obvious to others in the group until someone explains why they chose it. At the end of this clarification phase give everyone in the group three more dots each or tell them that they may each allocate up to three additional spots. They may choose to allocate any or all of their three additional dots (or spots) to an idea they haven't previously selected (though there is no compulsion to do so).

When all dots or spots have finally been allocated, rank the selected ideas in order of the number of dots or spots each has received. You can then take each in turn and evaluate its potential. One good way to do this is by using reverse brainstorming.

## Reverse brainstorming

Reverse brainstorming allows a group to test possible solutions by generating ideas about all the ways in which a proposed solution might go wrong. Use the dots and spots technique to identify the most likely-looking ideas and select the top-ranked three or so. (You could, of course, reverse brainstorm all the selected ideas if you have time.)

The rules and procedure are exactly the same as for normal brainstorming. The idea is to generate as many ideas as possible – no matter how implausible they may seem at first – in response to the stimulus: 'In what ways might [the idea] go wrong?' Write the stimulus question at the top of a flipchart sheet, remind the group of the rules for brainstorming, and set them off as before. As with normal brainstorming you can use silent incubation, wild ideas and excursions to stimulate ideas when they begin to flag. Repeat the process with each of the ideas you have selected for further examination until you have a comprehensive list of possible threats to the success of your ideas.

Then you're ready to turn your attention to evaluating these threats to your ideas and trying to find ways of neutralising them.

## Panic buttons

At the end of the reverse brainstorming session you will have generated another lists of ideas, this time of ways in which your solutions might go wrong. You need to distinguish those threats which are likely to prove a real concern from those which are neither serious nor probable. Panic buttons is a technique which makes this fun as well as effective.

Number each of the threats on the list the reverse brainstorming process has generated. Tell the group that you are going to read each item out in turn. Explain that you want each member of the group to press a panic button by calling out 'Beep!' each time you come to a threat which seems to them to need to be taken seriously. (If your organisational resources permit, each person could actually have a button attached to a real buzzer rather than just calling out: more noise, and more fun!) You should make a note of the number of each item for which someone pushed the panic button.

Once one or more people have pushed the panic button (whether for real or by calling out) the group should allocate points to that item. Each person can allocate up to ten points for seriousness, i.e. their evaluation of how much of a threat to success they believe this item to be, plus up to a further ten points for probability, i.e. how likely they think it is that this threat will arise in practice. Get everyone to write each of these two scores down separately – without any conferring or discussing with others – together with the item number to which they refer. Continue to read through the list with people pressing the panic button until all items have been read out.

Once you have come to the end of the list you need to collect scores for the 'beeped' items. Take each marked item in turn and collect the scores for that item from the group in two lists: first the seriousness score, then the probability one. When you have the scores for all the items, review the list. Identify the threats which have scored highest for both seriousness *and* probability: these are the ones which should be of highest concern.

Finally, use normal brainstorming to try to find ways to neutralise each of these threats to the success of your proposed solutions. As before, take each in turn and brainstorm (using the usual rules) in response to the stimulus: 'In what ways can we neutralise [threat]?'

By the end of this process you should not only have a much clearer idea of the nature and extent of the problems you face, but also a list of well-tested solutions which you can implement to combat them.

## OTHER TECHNIQUES

Although structured problem-solving techniques are important, there is a further set of techniques which, though different in intent, are equally valuable. Two techniques of particular benefit in empowerment are visualisation and metaphors.

143

### Visualisation

Visualisation is not a problem-solving technique: it's a problem-avoiding one. One important use of visualisation is to develop a vision to act as a motivating goal for your organisation, department or team. The use and value of such a vision was discussed in chapter 6.

The process is quite simple, if you are prepared to try. Even those who feel they have little imagination for such things can usually produce some kind of picture of a desirable future. Your vision doesn't have to be as abstract and unconnected with the practical realities of work as the Karmoy vision (see chapter 6) though, of course, it could be. It can be as practical and down to earth as you like, or as conceptual and ethereal as you wish. In fact it's important that you develop the right kind of vision for your own particular organisation or department. A very concrete one would perhaps be less effective in a highly-creative marketing consultancy than a more abstruse one. Similarly, most heavy engineering organisations would perhaps feel more comfortable with a more prosaic and literal picture. The form of the vision is also important. Is yours an organisation which would react better to a visual or a verbal expression of the vision? You need to choose the best form for your particular circumstances.

It's worth spending substantial time and effort on developing the vision, and it's also important to incorporate other people's ideas and aspirations. In a small team this means involving everyone. At the top of an organisation it may entail the senior management team working on developing the vision, but trying to ensure that they take soundings from as many people, at as many levels within the organisation, as possible, and then incorporating the ideas and feelings they have gleaned into the final vision.

144

A vision which is not shared is less effective than it might be. It's hard to impose a vision on someone else. Far better to try to ensure that the final vision contains and expresses shared ideas and ideals. You may find this easier to do with the help of an external facilitator who can help people to articulate their hopes and desires for the organisation, and who can assist in putting the vision together in its final form. Such a facilitator can help people to find appropriate images or words in which to express what is wanted, and to overcome any initial feelings of doubt about their ability to be creative in this way.

But whether you choose to work with an external facilitator or not, set aside at least a couple of hours for the task, and preferably more. People may take longer than you think to cast off inhibitions about expressing themselves in this way. You'll also need to explain the purpose of the activity and what you expect to happen. If you want to try to develop a pictorial or abstract vision, have available plenty of large (at least flipchart-size) sheets of paper and a variety of coloured pens and pencils. You needn't use paint, though it might help to free people's self-expression. Above all, present the activity as fun, as well as important. If you are too po-faced about it people will feel inhibited and embarrassed. You need to help people to find new ways of expressing ideas and feelings about the organisation and where it should be going.

Sharing laughter about your early efforts can be an important way to begin to share ideas and aspirations too.

The other kind of sharing which is important is the sharing of the final version of the vision. It is important also to find ways to express the vision you have developed so that it becomes meaningful and motivating for others as well as those who have developed it. If the final vision is in a verbal form, all staff need to receive a printed copy, together with an explanation. If it is pictorial or abstract, it might be shown first as a presentation slide accompanied by a verbal explanation of what it is about, and what it is intended to convey. Later, copies might be distributed or displayed prominently around the workplace. The important thing is that everyone should at least have access to the developed vision and, ideally, have shared in some way in its creation.

If you feel nervous about going the whole hog in this way, or feel that your staff would reject the notion as being altogether too airy-fairy, you can at least make a start by simply working verbally with your immediate team to try to come to a shared understanding of what you are all trying to achieve. You needn't even try to write down your initial efforts in this direction (though it would obviously help if you were to do so). Just discussing the issues can be of enormous value in helping you all to come to a shared understanding of goals and priorities. As a last resort you needn't involve others in the initial stages of developing vision at all, but work alone until you feel you have developed something to offer as a starting point for discussions.

But whether you are working alone or with others, or whether you are trying to develop a verbal or a pictorial vision, some useful questions to begin with include:

- What, ideally, would it feel like to work here?
- What is our most important goal?
- How could we tell if we had reached it?
- What other goals do we have?
- Which of these are most important?
- How could we tell if we had reached them?

145

- What values are important to us in our work?
- Why are these so important?
- What would total success in our endeavours look like?
- What would such success feel like?

You can probably think of others for yourself, depending on your own particular circumstances. If you are working alone, try to incorporate ideas that you think others might have too. Take time to develop a mental picture – as rich and detailed as you can – of your vision for the organisation.

If you find it hard to 'see' a picture at first, try warming up your mental muscles a little by picturing some simple objects. Close your eyes and imagine a rose in full bloom. Pick it up and smell the wonderful scent. Feel the sharpness of its thorns, and the velvety smoothness of the petals. Then imagine the petals slowly drooping, and finally dropping, one by one, brushing your hand as they fall.

Now imagine a speed-boat swooping across a bay. See the wash it creates as it swerves from side to side. Move your vision so that you are driving that speed-boat. See the wheel in front of you, then grasp it firmly. Look ahead to see where you are going. Hear the engines roar as you accelerate away. Now simply enjoy the sense of speed and power as you travel over the water, wherever you want to go.

Once you have begun to develop your vision, you can start to share it in pictures, in writing or simply by describing it to others. Whatever means you choose to develop and discuss your vision for the organisation, department or team, it needs eventually to become clear to all and shared by all. The form doesn't matter: the sharing does. Once you have broken the ice, you can work together to develop it further until you have a final vision which conveys to all what the organisation, department or team aims for and aspires to. Then everyone can feel truly empowered to act on their own initiative, confident that their actions are guided by a distinct and intelligible vision cf what they should be striving to achieve.

## Metaphors

One of the problems organisations often find when trying to talk about or paint a shared vision is the lack of a common language. People find they lack the necessary vocabulary to express and explain ideas about the organisation. They know what they want to express, but can't find the means to convey this to others. One way out of this difficulty is the use of metaphors.

People are sometimes nervous of the idea of using metaphors to talk about work issues, yet we all commonly use them all the time. We may describe an organisation as being like 'a well-oiled machine' or talk about a particular person who is prone to 'go for the jugular' in arguments. Often the use of such metaphors is reduced to the level of a cliché, as in these examples, but the carefully considered metaphor can help us to convey, in a simple but graphic form, quite complex ideas about organisations and what it is like to work in them.

147

A classic example of this is to liken an organisation to a car. Think for a moment. If your organisation were a car, what kind of car would it be? A Rolls-Royce perhaps? Or a slightly grubby family Volvo? A Ferrari? Or a clapped-out Ford Fiesta? And what kind of car *ought* it to be? What make and model should it be if it were to be the right kind of car/organisation to achieve its aims?

Most people cotton on to the idea very quickly and find it a very useful device not only to help them talk to one another about intangible issues regarding their hopes and aspirations, but also as a means for beginning to diagnose problems. For example, if you think the ideal car for your organisation's goals would be a hand-built Morgan, but your staff favour a mid-range Honda, you have uncovered some important differences in perception which need to be discussed and resolved if you are all to be able to drive in the same direction, let alone in the same kind of vehicle.

## TECHNIQUES AND EMPOWERMENT

These techniques are only examples of the kinds of activities which staff groups can undertake to help them share ideas about the organisation or department. You may know of others or you may find the services of a consultant useful in helping you and your staff to learn and use others. They are included here simply to stress the point that, given the right tools, systems and strategies (as well as the right attitudes), empowered staff can accomplish real improvements in organisational performance and achievement. Working together with your staff using such techniques can be a vital way to harness staff's knowledge and ideas and to consolidate their commitment to empowerment.

# 10

# Preparing to empower

**B**roadly speaking, there are two ways to tackle any organisational change, and the process of empowerment is no different. You can either tip-toe gently towards it or go for the 'big bang' approach. Each has its advantages and disadvantages. The gradual build-up approach can be less threatening to staff, who may not even realise that anything different is happening. If taken slowly enough it can help avoid the automatic resistance which is some people's natural response to any change. Some people are inherently more hesitant than others about accepting any change and their innate conservatism can often be circumvented by a sufficiently unhurried approach.

That's fine, of course, if you have the time to spare. But in some circumstances the need for change is so pressing that an unduly slow approach would risk too much else. Often organisations find themselves contemplating making major changes to the way they operate because of an equally major change in their circumstances, or because they are facing a significant transformation in their external environment. For them the choice may simply be to change quickly or to die. In these circumstances the 'big bang' approach is the only realistic option.

Going for a 'big bang' introduction has its own benefits too. It can generate a great deal of excitement, which can be an important factor in securing acceptance of a new idea. Excitement can also be critical at a time when the organisation is under threat or in the doldrums. Simply giving people an idea they can rally around can generate tremendous energy, confidence and enthusiasm, which can be important if your organisation is facing threats or severe competition. Offering people something they can cheer for can give an organisation just the fillip it needs to pull itself up by its own bootstraps.

At times of organisational stress it is also important to have some kind of unifying idea so that everyone feels they are pulling in the same direction. At the most basic level, staff may simply be grateful for the knowledge that management are actually trying to do something – anything! – rather than just wait for death to come. Even if your organisation is not under immediate threat a formal launch of a new organisational idea can be an effective strategy, not least because of the sense of renewal which it can offer. It also provides a better opportunity to explain not just what the change will be, but the reasons for it too. And it can be a good way to signal to your customers or clients that a change which will be of real benefit to them is happening. A softly-softly approach misses out on this important opportunity to involve your customers and convince them that you are putting them at the heart of your change strategy: that's too important a message to miss out.

150

In fact, of course, you can use a mixture of the two approaches. You can start with some gentle preparation and softening of the ground so that the 'big bang', when you are ready for it, has more chance of success. This is probably quite a sensible idea if you have the time for it. You need to be careful, though, that your slow build-up is actually slow enough or you'll fall between two stools. If your gentle introduction moves too fast you may stir up anxiety without having generated any compensatory excitement. So by all means take it cautiously at first, but plan to have a proper 'big bang' launch too. Before you can plan a big launch, however, you need to undertake some personal preparation.

# Personal preparation

It would be astonishing if, when contemplating what may be the biggest change you have ever made in your own management practice, you had no reservations at all. More than astonishing, it would be downright foolhardy. Such a major change is unlikely to be possible without some teething troubles, at least. So don't be concerned if you do have some worries at this stage. The important thing is to identify and deal with them so that you can approach the change with both confidence and realism.

Start by identifying your hopes and fears about the empowerment process. Make a list, starting with your fears. What are they? A typical list might include:

- staff will take advantage
- I'll lose control
- I won't know what is going on
- some of my staff simply aren't up to it
- we're not ready for this
- errors will increase
- staff will think I'm being weak
- my line manager will think I'm being weak

and so on.

Write your own list. Take your time over this, because it's important that you recognise clearly what it is about the idea that concerns you. You may even want to compile the list over several hours, or even days, adding items as they occur to you. Don't rush the process: take all the time you need.

## ELIMINATE THE NEGATIVE

Once you have completed your list, there's a useful technique you can apply to eliminate unnecessarily negative thoughts. It's called reversal. Just take each of your worries one by one and try a positive reversal. For example, instead of saying 'Staff will think I'm trying to take advantage of them', reverse this to 'Staff will realise that I'm trying to make full use of all their skills and knowledge'. You could turn 'I'll lose control' into 'Staff will be sharing the burden of responsibility', and so on. Concentrate on finding a positive way to look at each fear.

## ACCENTUATE THE POSITIVE

Now generate another list. This time write down all your hopes for the empowerment process. What do you want to achieve? What personal and organisational benefits do you hope it will bring? Again, take your time. Think as positively as you can.

When you have finished, add the list of positive items you derived from the reversal technique to your list of hopes. Now write it out attractively, or have it printed. This will be your own personal motivational tool. Pin it up in a prominent position or keep it close to hand so that you can find it easily. When the going gets tough (as it might) or when nagging doubts arise, take time to look again at your list to remind yourself of what it is that you are trying to achieve – and *will* achieve, if you just stick to your guns and to your convictions. And each time you do achieve one of your goals, tick it off on your list, so that you get a sense of progress. Alternatively, keep a running estimate of how much of each you have achieved so far, written as a percentage. You could even create a graph to show progress on each.

# Letting go

The next stage in the preparation process is letting go. It is essential to try to make some sensible decisions about what kinds of power and control can, and should, be devolved. What aspects of your work is it absolutely essential that you keep under your control? What can you afford to let go of? Remember, this question goes beyond simple delegation. You will be passing over power as well as responsibility.

Start by taking a large sheet of paper (a flipchart sheet is ideal).

You're going to create a chart with five columns in all, so make sure you allow enough space. (You might find you need to use the chart in landscape rather than portrait orientation.) Down the left-hand side, make a list of every aspect of your work that you feel you cannot let go of. In a second column, to the right of your list, add the reason you need to keep control of each aspect. Then add two more columns. In the first of these list the negative aspects of losing control in each area. Use the second to list the *positive* outcomes which might be achieved by *giving up* (not losing) control of these. There almost certainly are some. Try hard to find them.

Now look long and hard at your list. Which of these areas will you need to let go of if your staff are to be truly empowered? What will you need to pass on to them if they are going to be able to exercise their own initiative in pursuit of proper goals? Your positive list should help you identify these key issues. These are the areas where you will need to concentrate your energies during the empowerment process. Underline these in the first column. You might also find it helpful to make a separate list of them at some stage so that you can focus on them clearly.

153

Finally, add another column in which you identify the resources that need to be devolved with the power if empowerment is to work properly. Consider not just the physical and financial resources which might be needed but the knowledge, information, time, etc., that your staff will also need if they are to be enabled to function effectively in these areas. The final layout of your chart is shown in Fig. 10.1.

## PERSONAL BRAINSTORM

Once you have identified the key areas of power and control which you will need to devolve to your staff if empowerment is to work, you need to try to anticipate any possible problems so that you are forewarned and forearmed. With a little careful thought and planning you may be able to avoid them altogether.

As with any brainstorming session, you need to warm up your

creative 'muscles' before you start. So spend a minute or two trying to imagine a new machine for making tea. It can be as bizarre as you like (in fact, the more bizarre the better). What would such a machine dreamt up by Heath-Robinson look like? What about a Flintstones version? And a futuristic one?

Now start your personal brainstorm by asking yourself 'In what ways could the introduction of empowerment go wrong?' and then let your mind roam freely around the idea. Remember not to self-censor in any way. Try to generate as many responses as possible. Don't reject any idea, no matter how wild or improbable. Take your time. It's worth spending up to twenty minutes or so on this. Once you have generated your list, go back through it looking at each possible negative outcome in turn and asking yourself 'What will I do if this does happen?'. Try to find a positive solution for each. If you have space, jot your ideas for coping with the possible negative outcomes by the side of each.

154

The purpose of this is to help you anticipate any possible

| Can't let go | Reasons | Negatives | Positives | Resources |
|---|---|---|---|---|
|  |  |  |  |  |

**Fig. 10.1   Letting go**

difficulties so that you can avoid them wherever possible, and to show you that you will be able to cope even if they do happen.

## Planning for E-Day

Once you have completed your personal preparations it's time to start preparing the way for your staff. The first thing you need to do is to set a date for the launch of empowerment: E-Day. Choose a date at least a month away. Try to avoid a date which clashes with any other important organisational events, such as a major trade fair or a company open day. (Obviously, it's also a good idea to avoid Christmas and Easter or any other major religious festivals celebrated by your particular workforce.) If you can, avoid the peak holiday season too. It also makes sense to choose a time when you don't expect to be under any particular time or work pressure either. Block out several days either side of it too. Once you have chosen your date put it in your diary and regard it as sacrosanct. If anyone else keeps your diary for you, make it clear that these dates must be kept free at all costs. Now you're ready to start introducing the idea of E-Day to your staff.

155

All they need to know at this stage is that *something* will be happening on that date. If you have staff who are away from base for much of the time, make sure that they book the date you have selected as a base-day. Tell your staff that you are planning some changes and that this is the day on which all will be revealed. Explain that you need to have them all back at base on that day so that you can explain what it is all about. Build excitement: let them know that something unusual and worthwhile is planned, but don't let out too much information at this stage. Refer to your plans simply as E-Day.

It's important, though, to make sure that you are building interest and not anxiety. Convey a clear impression that what you have planned is a positive idea, and not a threat of any kind. There will always be some people, of course, who will automatically assume that what you are planning will bring bad news of some kind. There's probably not much you can do about them, if they're determined to take a pessimistic view. But you need to make it clear that you view their fears as being quite without foundation. Don't simply dismiss them: you need to take them seriously. But make it plain that you are confident that they will change their minds.

You may want to consider running what the advertising industry calls a 'teaser' campaign. This is a method of publicising a new product or service before its introduction by letting out tiny driblets of information or small clues in order to build interest as high as possible before the launch. Early versions of such teaser campaigns are the origin of the phrase 'watch this space'. You can use an adaptation of this idea to build positive interest too.

## CHOOSE YOUR CONFEDERATES

Unless yours is a very small team or department you will probably find it helpful at this stage to bolster yourself with the support of one or more confederates. Give some careful thought as to who these might be. Don't just plump automatically for your normal assistants or deputies. You may even decide to by-pass your formal seconds-in-command altogether. You should consider putting together a team which includes representatives from every level within your span of management so that you ensure that all types of staff are considered in the planning process This is an important step towards empowerment in itself. Empowerment is about harnessing the energies of everyone in the organisation. Putting together an E-Day team drawn from several organisational levels or areas of work could be a good way to start.

The people you choose should, above all, be likely to respond positively to the idea of empowerment, and to be able to give you both practical and moral support. If possible, you should also try to include some of the key opinion-formers. If you can get them on your side from the beginning then you'll be off to a flying start.

The other kind of person you should at least consider bringing into the E-Day team are the department mavericks, the ones who rock the boat and buck the trend. If you can get them on your side at the start they will be less tempted to react negatively as the process unfolds. You also need someone on the team who can stop you all becoming too complacent: mavericks are useful to fulfil that role. Empowerment is actually the kind of idea which is likely to appeal to those with independent minds and maverick tendencies, so if you involve them early they may turn out to be among your most powerful advocates.

## TRAIN YOUR TEAM

Once you have assembled your team you need to ensure that they have the skills and attitudes to back you up and provide the assistance and support you'll need as the empowerment process unfolds. This means explanations and training. If you lack training skills or confidence, or the time to use them, you might wish to consider bringing in an external consultant to help you with this process. But whether you undertake the training yourself or devolve it to someone else, it's essential that it happens.

157

The first thing to tackle is the idea of empowerment itself. Your E-Day team need to understand fully what empowerment means, and what it can offer. They need to know why you are planning to introduce the idea and how the organisation or department will benefit. It's particularly important that members of the team who have a management or supervisory role understand the changes that they will need to make in their own management style and for them to get some practice in using these new approaches. It's also essential that this early training is itself carried out in a manner appropriate to empowerment. This means that whoever is leading the group needs to be facilitative, rather than controlling, for that would send a very contradictory message. Even if you are confident that you can do this (and it's neither as simple nor as common a skill as you might suppose) there may still be some benefit in using an external facilitator rather than run the sessions yourself. If you are prepared to learn together with your team this is a strong reinforcement of the empowerment message.

Above all, your team need to know what's in empowerment for them. Explain it as clearly as you can and deal honestly with their questions. Once they understand it you may find it helpful to run a 'hopes and fears' session. You'll be running these for the rest of your staff on E-Day itself, so this is a good opportunity to practice. If you're nervous, or not sure of your ability to run a training group using a facilitative approach, use a consultant to run these early sessions so that you can see how it is done.

Pin up two flipchart sheets, headed 'Hopes' and 'Fears' respectively. Then either ask people to call out their hopes and fears about empowerment or give them pens and let them write their ideas on the sheets themselves. Encourage people to be completely open and honest. Stress that you really need to know how they feel. Make sure they understand that you will treat both kinds of feelings seriously.

Then talk the group through both lists. Are their hopes capable of being realised through empowerment? If not, they need to understand which ones are unrealistic. Equally, you need to emphasise those hopes which you and they might reasonably expect to see happen. Spend time talking through those too, to fix them in people's minds as something to aim for. Now take the fears list. Again, some will be realistic and others not. Take even the wildly improbable worries seriously, and talk them through until people begin to accept that they are probably unfounded. Where realistic concerns persist, discuss how likely these are, and how they can be avoided or coped with if they should occur. Aim throughout to be both positive and realistic. People's fears only increase if you dismiss them too easily. Treat them seriously and they may be dispelled, especially if people can see that they can be dealt with even if they do come about.

Once people have accepted the idea of empowerment and (if you've dealt sympathetically but positively with their concerns) become enthusiastic about it, you need to teach them some of the problem-solving techniques discussed in the previous chapter.

You might find it helpful to make the empowerment process and E-Day itself the focus of the problem-finding phase. That way you not only train staff to use the techniques but also begin to use them to achieve real, practical results to help you introduce empowerment successfully.

You may need to hold several team meetings to cover the whole process, so be prepared to teach and use only one technique at a time. It's far better to allow people to become fully familiar with using such approaches (especially if they are unfamiliar) than simply to rush through them on a 'here's one, and here's another' basis. You need to help people make the techniques part of their own problem-solving repertoire so that their use becomes second nature. There are two main reasons for this. Firstly, its only when we become fully familiar and comfortable with such techniques that we actually use them. It's no good people simply knowing that such approaches to solving problems exist. They need to feel confident about applying them in a range of contexts, and that only comes with practice.

Secondly, the team that you have put together will act as both catalysts and supporters for the changes you propose to introduce, particularly if you have drawn them from all organisational levels. Not only can they then use these techniques *in situ* but they can train others to do the same. If you are attempting to introduce empowerment on a large scale throughout an entire organisation of any size, you may also need to select and prepare a specialist training team. (This is discussed in the next chapter). But in a smaller organisation or department your E-Day team will be sufficient to fulfil this role. However, even if you do plan to set up a special training team it's still important that your E-Day team are fully competent in using problem-solving techniques. This will help to ensure that they are not only to able to give informed and enthusiastic support for their use, but also that they are able to act as role models and exemplars of their effectiveness. Furthermore, they can be invaluable in the next stage of the process: planning E-Day itself.

## INVOLVE YOUR TEAM

The next chapter will discuss ideas for the implementation of E-Day and beyond. But it's important that you don't simply impose such ideas on your team. Involve them fully in all planning from now on. It rather defeats the object, after all, to tell people you intend to empower them, and this is how you will do it! Remember: from now on people will notice not just what you say about empowerment but how you act. Empowerment needs to start with your E-Day team. If you can't (or won't) empower *them*, you certainly won't be able to empower anyone else either.

So this is the first real test of your own skills and resolve, and one you will almost certainly fail! It's almost inescapable. Even if you have been trying to introduce the idea slowly so far it's unlikely that old habits will die easily or quickly. Why should they? It's by the exercise of the old management skills of leadership and control that you came to be in a position to empower people in the first place. You're probably very good at using these skills to achieve organisational goals. Giving them up won't be easy or quick.

But don't be disheartened, or give up at the first fall. Talk to your team about the difficulties you experience and enlist their positive support in helping you to overcome any setbacks or back-sliding on your part. Remember that if they too have some kind of managerial or supervisory role they're going to find it hard to adopt a new way of working too. So be open about your own difficulties and encourage them to give you clear feedback on how you're doing. They need to be able to let you know if you are slipping back into old habits of command and control. If they see you genuinely striving to achieve personal change, not only will they be more understanding and accepting of occasional slip-ups in this direction but you'll also be offering them a positive role model for the time when they too will have to relinquish some of their own control.

So take the opportunity offered by planning E-Day to involve your team fully in the process and make good use of their particular local knowledge of the organisation or department. It's a good chance for you and for them to begin to develop and practice skills of sharing ideas and power in an empowered organisation.

161

# 11

# E-Day and after

In chapter 10 the need to involve your E-Day team fully in the planning process was stressed. Nothing suggested here should be thought to contradict that. What follows are some recommendations which you and your team need to consider in relation to your own organisation and its context.

The important thing is that your E-Day should launch the idea of empowerment in a way which is acceptable to your staff. It must convince them that it offers real benefits not just to the organisation (though this is, of course, important) but to each of them as individuals and group members too. One possible approach is to run a launch meeting, or a series of meetings if yours is a large organisation and you are attempting an organisation-wide empowerment programme. These meetings have several purposes:

- to inform people of the proposed changes
- to introduce them to the basic principles of empowerment
- to explain why you think it is important to introduce empowerment
- to explain the potential benefits of empowerment for both individuals and the organisation
- to give staff the opportunity to begin to practise empowered behaviour.

The success of these meetings is crucial to the ultimate success of the empowerment programme.

# The launch

No matter how you intend to launch the empowerment programme, it must happen with as much of a fanfare as you can
contrive. Even if you are only introducing the idea to a small team
you need to build as much excitement into the process as you can.
The process described here is based on using a series of meetings,
but if you and your E-Day team want to use a different approach
then make sure whatever you plan incorporates the same principles.

Start with a meeting for all your staff, preferably off-site but
within normal working hours. Let people know well in advance
when and where it will be held, and build excitement about the
idea. If you can't get all your staff in one place at the same time,
either because the organisation is simply too big or because yours
is a twenty-four-hour operation, run a series of such meetings one
after the other, preferably on the same day. (Run them through
the night too if that is the best way to reach your night staff.)
Spread the meetings into the next day only if there are simply too
many to fit into just one.

If you are holding more than one meeting, make sure that every
single person in the organisation or department has a specified
time to attend. And that does mean *everyone*, even part-timers,
cleaners, short-contract staff, etc. You need to be serious about
this or you won't succeed. It's also essential that staff of all grades
and from all parts of the organisation are present at each meeting.
If you hold separate meetings for senior, middle and junior
managers, supervisors and staff you are sending a message which
directly contradicts that of empowerment. Such status differen-
tials have no place in an empowering organisation.

It is also essential that any interval between the meetings should
be kept as short as possible. If you allow too large an interval, the
gossiping will begin and the rumour mill will start to churn out its
usual stream of half-truths and misinformation. The only
exception to this rule is the possible need to hold a final, supple-
mentary launch meeting a week or two later to catch those who

163

were absent due to illness, holidays, etc. So keep an accurate record of attendance at all meetings. If people miss the first batch, make sure they attend the later 'catching up' meetings for absentees.

If you can't arrange the meeting within people's normal working hours, pay staff for attending: it'll be worth it. It's also worth spending some effort and cash on the venue if you can. Choose a pleasant room, or make an ordinary workspace seem special with hired potted plants and so on. You want people to see that this is the beginning of something special for the organisation and for them too. Serve tea or coffee: it's a small investment compared to the message it sends. Do everything you can to make the occasion seem special and exciting.

## 164   RUNNING THE MEETINGS

Use the meetings to sell the idea of empowerment to your staff, not just tell them what it will entail. Sell the *benefits* which empowerment can bring. Stress the benefits for them, for customers and for the organisation as a whole. Be honest, too, about the benefits for management. If you don't then people will tend to be cynical and assume the worst: that this is just a way to dump unwanted responsibility on them. Stress the opportunities it offers to managers to have access to the knowledge and skills which staff have and which they have too often ignored or failed to recognise in the past. Point out that too much internal fire-fighting can lead to too little external fire-spotting, which is what managers need to do if the organisation is to avoid disasters. If management are to become the strategic thinkers they are paid to be, then they need access to the local knowledge which staff hold, and the space to work with staff to develop strategic vision. Empowerment offers both of these.

## DEVELOP A SHARED VISION

One way to involve staff in empowerment right from the very beginning is to give them the opportunity to share in the development of the vision which will guide the organisation through the empowerment process. Ways of running an envisioning session were explored in chapter 9. If you are introducing empowerment on an organisation-wide basis, bear in mind that running visioning sessions at the launch meetings doesn't stop you running further sessions with your own immediate team prior to or after the launch sessions. You can and should try to incorporate the visions developed at these launch meetings into the vision which you and your team develop.

If your meetings involve large groups of staff you will probably need help to run the visioning sessions. You can use either outside consultants or your E-Day team (or both) for this. The precise way in which you introduce the idea will also have to be modified to suit your organisation and the kind of people who work there. In a small creative advertising agency you can probably afford to dive straight in to the visual imagining stage. A larger, more conventional or traditional company such as a bank or manufacturing company may need to use a modified approach to avoid staff rejecting the idea out of hand. But beware of simply assuming that your staff are too conservative for some of the more unusual and imaginative approaches: you'd be amazed at what people will try if you present it to them in the right way. Present the idea as both fun and functional, and most people will join in.

165

If you are running a large meeting you need to divide people into groups of between five and nine. The groups should be as mixed in composition as possible. Try to avoid groups whose members are all drawn from the same work group or even department, and try to ensure that managers and supervisors are spread evenly too. Ideally, each of the groups will have its own facilitator, but experienced facilitators may be able to run more than one group each by moving between them.

Then make sure that everyone understands the instructions. In particular, they need to understand that you are asking them to create a vision of an ideal – not necessarily an immediately achievable – state of affairs. You need them to dream a little. Then display a list of prompt questions (see chapter 9) prominently somewhere, and make sure that each group also has a copy of them. If you are using a 'safer' approach simply ask people to discuss the questions and write down their answers. If you want to take a few risks, get people to close their eyes and literally envision the answers. They can then either discuss these in the group or, if you really want to open up people's creative responses, draw or even paint a joint vision within the group.

Allow at least half an hour for this process, excluding explanations and instructions. This may also be a good point at which to serve refreshments. Aim for an atmosphere of relaxed playfulness but serious intent. Laughter is almost certainly a sign that things are going well. Try to find ways also to keep groups that finish earlier than others involved until everyone has finished. You might do this by arranging for a facilitator to talk to those group, perhaps encouraging them to develop their vision still further; or you might encourage two or more groups to share their ideas.

When all groups seem to have achieved a completed vision you need to share them in some way. Drawings or paintings should be displayed so that everyone can see them. Written visions should be read out by a representative of the group. Such occasions commonly create laughter as well as interest, so don't try to suppress this. Even a jokey response this may express as many important truths and ideas as more serious offerings. No matter what form the visions take it's essential that you share them and treat them with respect. This also means that they shouldn't simply be discarded once they have been shared. You should ensure that they are collected and kept carefully. Not only are they an important resource for further development of the organisation's vision, but they provide a valuable record of staff's ideas at the start of the empowerment process. It's also a good idea to spend some time after the final launch meeting trying to encapsulate the major themes from all the visions and feeding these back to everyone in some way. You might try to consolidate them into one (or even more than one) detailed verbal vision and give everyone a copy. Or you might employ an artist to create a visual consolidation of the main ideas, whether they were originally expressed verbally or visually. (If your staff includes someone with the talent to do this, then so much the better.) Then display the resulting artwork prominently, or distribute copies if you can. (Large colour photographs would work well.) You might also consider disseminating the resulting vision still further by sending copies of it to major customers, or by including it in the organisation's promotional material. If the final product is visual the local press or television companies may even be interested in it too.

## HOPES AND FEARS

Another useful activity for the launch meetings is a Hopes and Fears session. You can run this in much the same way as the one you held with your E-Day support team. The groups should remain the same as for the visioning session. Each group needs a flipchart pad and stand, and marker pens. Make sure that everyone understands what is required. Make particularly certain that people understand how this session differs from the visioning one. That session involved imagining an ideal and even idealised future. The focus of this session needs to be more immediate and realistic. The groups should list all the hopes and fears they have in relation to the empowerment process. Emphasise the need to be open in their views. Assure them that you intend to use their lists to help you manage the empowerment process and avoid the problems that they may be concerned about. Then allow at least twenty minutes for the groups to generate their lists. As before, if some groups finish early, talk to them and encourage them to generate more ideas.

Once all the groups have generated a list, combine each group with another and ask them to produce a joint list which includes all the individual items from each group but which has eliminated any duplications. Then (if numbers permit) ask each of these joint groups to combine with another and repeat the process. Finally, share the combined lists with the entire group.

167

Then debrief the session. Explain that the combined 'Hopes' and 'Fears' lists will be used to help guide the empowerment process. Then choose one or two of the fears you think least likely to be a real problem. Explain why you think this is so. But don't dismiss these ideas: take them seriously, but reassure people that they are unlikely to occur. Where some fears seem to you to be justifiable, talk about these too. Show that you share their concerns and, if possible, say how you intend to try to avoid them if at all possible.

Finally, take some of the items from the 'Hopes' list that you believe may be realisable through the empowerment process. Explain why you think these will happen and how. Tell people that the 'Hopes' list will be continually referred to as the empowerment process gets under way as a means of checking progress. Then stress again the potential for overall benefits that empowerment offers and bring the meeting to a close, trying to finish on a note of high optimism.

# Follow-up

Once E-Day is over and you have informed all of your staff about the changes you plan there remain some important things to do. One of the most important of these is to tell your customers what you hope will be happening. It's easy, by this stage, to lose sight of the fact that one of the main reasons for starting the process at all is to provide a better service to your customers (and, of course, to gain competitive advantage by doing so). You are not trying to empower your staff out of sheer benevolence and kindness of heart. You are investing all this time, effort and money so that your organisation or department will achieve real improvements in the service or the product it provides.

So make sure that your customers know this is what they can expect. Doing this is not just a good publicity opportunity (though it's certainly that too) but an important motivational device for you and your staff. If you have promised your customers that they will be able to look forward to real improvements then this will provide a powerful incentive to ensure that this really does happen. This applies just as much to those of you who serve only internal customers. Too often we forget that service or administrative departments also have customers, and that these customers are just as important as any other kind. If every part of an organisation gave excellent service and perfect products to its internal customers then the overall efficiency and productivity of the whole organisation would be vastly improved. So don't just assume that because you don't provide a service or product directly to the public or to some other kind of external purchaser, you don't have customers: you do. Everyone does. But do you know who yours are?

If not, take some time to identify your customers. You need to let them know that you are taking steps to try to improve what you provide just as much as any direct service, retailer or supplier does. And to do that you need to know who they are. Remember, you may not actually provide a tangible product or direct service but you still have customers. You may provide advice to individuals or information to other parts of the organisation instead: these are your customers. Let them know what improvements they can expect.

169

If you serve internal customers then the jungle telegraph will certainly have made sure that they know that *something* is going on, especially once you have held your launch meetings. But you can't afford to let them receive just hearsay information which is only partly correct at best and perhaps even downright misleading. You need to ensure that they receive a message which is as positive as the one your staff received. So find a way to let them know clearly what you are up to and what you expect the benefits to be. Exactly how you do this will depend, of course, on the kind of organisation you work for and the nature of the product or service you provide, but some possibilities include sending memos, putting slips in pay packets, holding a briefing meeting for key personnel, and announcing your plans in the company newsletter or magazine. Choose the method which best suits your own particular circumstances.

If you do actually serve external customers of some kind you need to let them know what you're trying to do. Again, the method you choose will depend on who those customers are and the best way to reach them. In a small service or retailing organisation one effective way is to display attractive posters explaining the idea of empowerment in simple terms and outlining what your customers can expect from the process and any changes for the better that they may notice. Larger concerns may wish to consider advertising or direct mailings to reach their wider customer base. If you provide a business-to-business service or sell products to other organisations you may need to provide your direct service or sales staff with special training so they can explain the ideas behind empowerment to your clients and customers. You may also wish to include some kind of explanatory statement in your catalogue, or other sales or promotional literature that you distribute.

But no matter who your customers are or how you decide to reach them with the message, the message itself needs to be the same: empowerment is a change for the better which will improve the service you offer or the products you supply. Tell them to expect to see positive results and make sure your staff know that is what you have told them. That way everyone has a real incentive to achieve the improvements you have promised that empowerment will provide.

## Making it work

If you have got your preparation and planning right you will have ensured that your staff and even your customers are now as keen as you are to see empowerment work. Now you need to start taking practical steps to ensure that it does.

The first step should be to set clear boundaries for staff's discretion to act on their own initiative. You have already examined your own willingness to give up some areas of power and responsibility. It's time to put this into practice. Staff need to know that these boundaries are to be redrawn and exactly where the new boundaries will be. So the next thing to do is to involve your staff in negotiating where those boundaries should be. You need to talk to them about removing blocks to full organisational efficiency and ways to achieve wholly satisfied customers. Depending on your own particular circumstances and those of your staff you may need to negotiate the widening or even removal of boundaries with individuals one at a time, or with groups of staff or their representatives. Either way you may find that you and your staff don't quite see eye to eye at first over where the boundary lines should be drawn. Chapter 7 discussed the difficulties you might face if staff are reluctant to take on more responsibility, but what if your staff actually want *more* than you had originally intended to devolve?

171

The first thing to be said is that you should regard this as an encouraging sign. Your staff have obviously been convinced about the potential benefits of empowerment and are keen to be fully involved. You should not dent that enthusiasm. On the other hand, you may still be feeling a bit jittery about the idea and reluctant to let go of too much, at least to begin with. You need to find some workable compromise which will not demotivate your staff or lessen their enthusiasm for the idea of empowerment, but which will still allow you to feel confident that it won't all go horribly wrong. This will involve some careful negotiations and keeping your mind as open as you can about the possible outcomes.

You need first to try to re-assess the level of risk with which you feel comfortable. You may need to acknowledge that your worries probably have more to do with your own sense of insecurity than with any objective assessment of your staff's ability to cope. If so, you need to look again at the boundaries you had intended to set and see if you might risk setting them a little wider or further out than you feel entirely comfortable with at first. It is also very important that your staff should understand why you feel so anxious if they are not to suspect you of a lack of real commitment to the idea of full empowerment. So talk openly to your staff. Own up to your anxieties and the reasons for them, stressing your own nervousness and not any lack of competence on their part. The chances are that they will be sympathetic to your concerns.

On the other hand, your staff may have genuinely overestimated the difficulties involved in what they propose. If this really is the case, then you may need to explain exactly why what they propose is not really feasible. They may take some convincing. If yours has been a rather paternalistic organisation until now, staff who are newly empowered may be rather like adolescents who have only recently left childhood. In both cases there may be a tendency to oscillate between unrealistic demands for independence and equally vehement insistence that the adult/manager take over control and responsibility again.

172

If you find this is happening both you and your staff will just have to let nature and empowerment take their course. With experience and goodwill on both sides each is likely to become a little more realistic. If you are faced with such difficulties it might be worth keeping in mind the comment once made to a former colleague of mine who was bemoaning the typically-adolescent behaviour of his teenage sons. Complaining to his ex-wife about this he asked rhetorically when on earth they were ever going to leave adolescence behind and grow up. 'They will eventually,' said their mother. 'After all, you're beginning to.'

So get together with your staff and negotiate with them to agree a level of acceptable risks on your side and reasonable scope for initiative on theirs. Spend some time and effort on jointly planning ways to monitor these changes frequently so that you feel comfortable that any problems will be picked up quickly. That way you may feel more confident about letting go a little bit more. Above all, keep reminding yourself that the more you can share responsibility with your staff the more time and thought you can spare for strategic management. It really will be worth it once it begins to work.

# Putting it into practice

One important early step you can take to help ensure the success of your empowerment programme is to set up a system of regular Process Meetings. These need to be quite separate from and additional to any normal management meetings you may also hold. This isn't just a case of one more set of pointless meetings to fit into an already overcrowded schedule. You really do need some kind of forum at which issues relating to empowerment can be discussed. The purpose of these Process Meetings is to provide just such a forum, in which all can freely and openly share ideas, opinions and feelings about empowerment and the changes in working practices it demands.

You should aim to hold Process Meetings for all staff at least weekly for the first month, then monthly after that – forever. If your empowerment programme involves more than about ten staff you may need to set up several such meetings. Every single member of your staff needs to belong to a Process group, and the best size of group is from around half a dozen members to about ten or so. Where possible and appropriate you should try to base Process group membership on the groups from the launch meetings.

It's essential that neither you nor any other manager should dominate these meetings or play a prominent role in them in any way (though its equally essential that all managers, including you, should belong to a process group). Aim to be simply another participant. After the first (or first few) meetings, it is a good idea for staff to share responsibility for facilitating the meeting on a rota basis, with you and your fellow managers simply taking your turn like anyone else. This ensures that you won't be in a position to exert undue influence on the conduct or content of the meetings. Not only that, it actually frees you to be an equal participant in them, and gives you the chance to speak your mind as openly as anyone else.

Process Meetings should not have a formal agenda. Their purpose is simply to provide an open forum for free discussion. The role of

173

the facilitator is not to control or direct the meeting in any way but merely to ensure that participants know when and where the meeting will take place, and to ensure that facilities are available. Beyond that the facilitator's role is simply to try to ensure that everyone has a chance to express his or her views and that no one regularly dominates the proceedings. When such meetings are established and are working well they should function for the most part as leaderless groups. If you and your staff are not used to holding this type of informal, agenda-less meeting you may need some training or guidance in how they work. In any case everyone needs to know the basic rules and principles on which they need to function.

Process Meetings need to be based on trust between

- manager and staff
- staff and manager
- staff and one another

if they are to be productive and worthwhile. This means that preserving confidentiality about what is said is important, as are complete honesty and openness.

Although there will be no formal agendas it is useful to have a set of formal 'rules' for such meetings, based on the rules of assertiveness. These include:

- comment only on behaviour, not personality
- say 'I feel . . .', not 'You are . . .'
- everyone owes it to everyone else to say openly and clearly what they think, not hide it
- critique (i.e. *positive* criticism, aimed at giving feedback and seeking solutions) is welcome, but criticism (i.e. *negative* comments, aimed at blaming and offering no solutions) is not
- staff and managers both need to be able to critique one another's performance in terms of empowered behaviour.

It is essential that all participants know about these rules and recognise the importance of keeping to them.

A useful focus for Process Meetings, especially in the early stages of the empowerment programme, is the Hopes and Fears lists generated at the launch meetings. It might be a good idea to refer to these at every Process Meeting till all (reasonable) hopes are met and fears have all been resolved. The groups might continue to add to the lists at each Process Meeting if necessary and might also review the 'achieved' items on the Hopes list from time to time to ensure that problems have not re-arisen.

Another useful focus might be resource management and the extent to which staff empowerment is adequately supported by the provision and allocation of time, finance, training, materials, etc. These topics should not be placed on a formal agenda. Groups should simply be aware of the need to discuss such issues, plus others which they may identify for themselves, from time to time.

175

Process groups allow everyone to reflect on how the empowerment programme is going and to examine and, if necessary, reset boundaries. They open the process up to shared examination and help to ensure that staff and managers really do share responsibility for its success. By providing a forum in which issues and problems can be discussed many of the potential difficulties can be circumvented and staff's continuing commitment to the principles and practice of empowerment ensured. Above all they are a very practical and simple way to open up management agendas and issues to staff scrutiny so that true empowerment can become a practical reality.

# 12

# How's it going?

Once you've set the process of empowerment in train you need to turn your attention to monitoring the process and evaluating its success. You'll want to be sure that all your efforts have really produced results, and that these results were worth the effort. But how can you tell if empowerment is working, and achieving the successes you hoped for? How can you tell how it's going?

There are a number of factors which indicate the success of empowerment. You'll know it's going well if:

- staff seem happier (once initial teething problems are over)
- *you* feel confident and generally happy with what's happening
- performance standards have at least been maintained, and preferably improved
- errors and complaints have fallen
- staff absences are reduced
- staff turnover is lower
- staff are increasingly able and willing to offer constructive criticism of management
- managers (including you) are increasingly able and willing to accept constructive criticism from staff
- staff/management relationships are warmer and more open
- customers/clients are expressing greater satisfaction
- managers are spending less time on fire-fighting, and more on strategic planning

and so on. The more of this kind of evidence you can see the more confident you can be that you are achieving success.

On the other hand, you may not yet be achieving the fullest possible benefits from empowerment because you haven't implemented it fully enough. You'll know you've not yet gone far enough if staff are asking for still more responsibility and even, perhaps, seem on the verge of revolt. Remember: empowering staff is a little like helping adolescents to grow up. You may need to relax the boundaries of your own control beyond limits with which you feel totally comfortable. If you begin to slacken the boundaries so that you raise expectations of greater freedom then fail to let go sufficiently, you may provoke the same kind of rebelliousness in your staff that over-protective or over-controlling parents provoke in their adolescent children. So if you're having problems with staff being unco-operative or obstructive, don't just assume that empowerment isn't working or that you've gone too far. It *could* be because you've not gone far enough.

177

But what if it has all gone terribly wrong? What if the result of all your efforts is not empowered staff and happy customers but a horrible mess? What might have gone wrong and how can you put it right?

# Coping with CHAOS

When evaluating the success of your empowerment programme you need to look out for signs of CHAOS:

- Confusion
- Hassles
- Anger
- Obstruction
- Stasis

and, if you find evidence of any of these, you need to take immediate steps to overcome these setbacks. Even if you are not actually facing chaos, the CHAOS acronym can help you to be on the alert for any problems which may begin to arise. Tackle these problems as soon as you spot the least sign of them beginning so that real chaos is averted.

## CONFUSION

If people seem to be confused about what to do or about what is expected of them you need to remedy this. They may be confused in a number of different ways and about a number of different issues. These can be thought of as falling into a number of categories. You may need to sort out

- goals
- roles
- holes
- souls

if confusion is to be banished.

Let's take goals first. Do people know what they should be aiming for? Did you succeed in developing a shared vision? Even if you did, should you perhaps review this to see if any changes or strengthening are needed? It cannot be stressed too often or too strongly that unless people know what is expected of them and what they should be striving to achieve they will lack both direction and motivation. Make sure that everyone is pulling in the same direction, and that the direction is right. This may require a radical reassessment of overall aims or strategy or just a minor realignment. Either way, talk to your staff. Find out if they know clearly what they are aiming for. If they do, is that where they should be aiming? Spend time reassessing goals and communicating any changes clearly if you find confusion here.

Now what about roles? Do your staff understand the range and limitations of the roles they should be playing? Is there confusion about the boundaries of their power and responsibility? Do they understand how their roles relate to yours and to one anothers?' If they are not clear about the extent of their devolved power you need to renegotiate this until both you and they have a clear picture of where your respective levels of power lie.

What holes might there be in the empowerment process? Are there any omissions or gaps in the systems and procedures which you are using to support empowerment? Is there a lack of information somewhere? Look carefully at your systems and strategies, especially those to do with communication. Any holes in these could be adding to people's confusion.

Finally, what about souls? Are there any particular individuals who are finding it hard to cope with empowerment, perhaps because they're not sure what it is all about? Is there anyone who is continuing to resist the idea and who is sowing the seeds of confusion in others? Check to see if you can spot anyone who seems to be struggling to accept or cope with the idea of empowerment. Talk to them and try to find out where the problem lies. Then stress the potential personal benefits it could bring if they give it a chance.

179

## HASSLES

Is there interpersonal or interdepartmental friction anywhere? If so you need to tackle it. This kind of hassle sometimes occurs when boundaries of power and responsibility between individuals or groups are either not sufficiently clear or set in the wrong place. If you are aware of a pattern of hassles between specific individuals or groups you need to bring them together to renegotiate boundaries around their respective fields of operation. Try to reach agreement so that each person or group feels they have been treated fairly.

## ANGER

The most common kind of anger which occurs in empowerment is anger that you or other managers have refused the role of Magic Helper. People can become very cross when they feel they are being forced to stand on their own feet. The worst kind of anger of this kind, paradoxically, may occur when people *have* taken a decision of their own and it has gone wrong. Thrashing around for someone to blame, they may fix on you on the grounds that you should somehow have prevented them from making the error. No, it is neither rational nor reasonable, but it does happen. The only thing you can do in these circumstances is to remain calm yourself but refuse to accept ownership of other people's mistakes. Try to help them see how they can learn from the errors. Eventually this kind of error becomes more rare as people begin genuinely to accept responsibility for their own actions and decisions. It takes time, but it does happen, as long as you can retain the courage to keep rejecting the Magic Helper role.

## OBSTRUCTION

Some people, however, will go beyond anger to deliberate obstructiveness. There are really only two ways to cope with this. You can either persuade them to join you or you can beat them. The first is obviously the preferable option. Chapter 7 discusses some positive ways in which you can overcome people's doubts and resistance. In the end, however, you may have to accept that one or two people simply will not be won round. Your only option then is to limit their influence on others and let them be. If you can, try to encourage a collective view of such obstructors as people who are more to be pitied for not being able to cope with the demands of empowerment than blamed for being deliberately awkward.

The other kind of obstruction which causes problems lies not in people but in the systems they use. The most common and prob- lematical of these are obstructions in communications systems. If your empowerment process doesn't seem to be going as well as it should, look out for obstructions or hold-ups in whatever com- munications systems you have set up. Remove any you find. For example, if you are a senior manager you may discover that supervisors or more junior managers are acting as blocks rather than as conduits of communications between you and front-line staff: a very common problem, and one you need to find ways to overcome or bypass. Pay special attention also to horizontal communication systems. Obstructions here can cause major problems. Make sure your staff can communicate freely with one another and with other teams or departments.

## STASIS

You may be beginning to think that if trying to empower people brings all these problems then it might be best not to attempt it at all, or only in a very small and modified sort of way. In fact stasis – lack of movement – is often a problem too. Stasis is often based on fear: fear that any movement or change will bring disaster. It's a little like finding yourself on a narrow plank over a deep ravine, afraid to move forward and afraid to move back. But if a tiger were coming after you you'd soon move forward! Look again. There is just such a tiger, and its stripes spell the word 'competitors'.

181

No matter whether the customers you serve are external or internal to your organisation your survival depends on keeping them happy. Managers in all sorts of organisations, large and small, whether industrial, commercial or public sector, are increasingly coming to realise that competitive edge is the key to survival. Organisations which offer a better product will outperform others. But those which can provide excellence of service as well will perform best of all. Your organisation's very existence may depend on its ability to align staff behaviour with corporate goals of service excellence. Stasis in such circumstances is simply not an option for any company which wants to survive. Empowerment improves customer service by accessing and harnessing the close-to-the-customer skills of an organisation's front-line staff. Empowerment then ensures that these staff have the freedom and support they need to provide first-rate customer service with maximum efficiency and minimum delay by removing unnecessary organisational blocks and barriers. It's a simple but highly effective approach, requiring only minor investment yet producing major returns.

So no matter what difficulties there may be in establishing

empowerment as a dominant management strategy within your organisation, the risks of *not* attempting it are far higher still. Empowerment isn't the real problem. Stasis is.

## Empowering customers and clients

The final check you need to undertake when assessing the success of your empowerment programme is with your customers or clients. Do *they* see a difference? Are they receiving the service they want from your organisation or department? More to the point, have you empowered them to tell you what they need from you?

In addition to empowering your staff you need to find ways of extending the boundaries of empowerment and getting closer to your customers. They need to be able to reach into your organisation to communicate their needs and you need to be able to reach out to find out more about them. Customer satisfaction surveys, buyer panels, open days, etc., all help to establish a framework in which you and your customers work together to ensure that you meet their needs. You renegotiated your boundaries of power to enable you to make full use of your staff's knowledge, skill and experience. Now you need to begin a similar process with your customers, empowering them to tell you exactly what they want from your organisation or department and its staff.

Empowering your staff is only the first step. Only when you empower your customers and clients too will you have mobilised empowerment to deliver full competitive advantage to your organisation. And that – after all – is what empowerment is all about.

And finally . . .

In the end, the final question must be: does empowerment work? Most importantly, can it actually bring real competitive advantage? Yes, you and your staff should feel greater personal satisfaction at work. Yes, staff turnover and stress should be reduced. Yes, you should become more free to think strategically and make fuller use of your management skills. But, important though these are, such advantages are not enough to justify the time and trouble of introducing empowerment. Most managers will also want to be convinced that there will be some kind of bottom-line pay-off too. So can *you* look forward to real competitive advantage for your organisation as a result of empowerment? Well, others have achieved it.

The most dramatic example of this is perhaps the Brazilian company Semco, a producer of dishwashers, pumps and cooling units. At a time of world recession, when Brazil itself has a national economy struggling to surmount debt and conquer hyper-inflation, Semco has no debts and exports nearly a quarter of its output. Since introducing its ambitious company-wide empowerment programme it has seen a fivefold increase in profits *in real terms* and has achieved a sevenfold increase in productivity: enough, surely, to satisfy even the toughest bottom-liner. Perhaps that's why nearly one in three of America's top Fortune 500 companies has sent representatives to Semco to find out how they do it. The 'secret', they discovered, is the company's wholehearted commitment to empowerment.

183

At Semco, everyone shares in the decision-making about company direction and development, right down to choosing new sites and factory layout. Every single member of staff has access to the company's books, and financial decisions are shared, including how much to pay out as profit-share and how much to invest. A quarter of the workforce currently set their own salaries, and in future, everyone will do. Staff come to work and leave when they choose, and only about a third are directly employed at the factory. The rest are mainly former staff who have set up as independent suppliers or consultants, or have opted to work from home. Managers have their performance rated by their staff every six months, and the results are displayed for all to see. Those who score consistently poor ratings are expected to leave the company. The next stage is for staff to be able to elect their immediate manager too, an idea designed to 'stop accidents before they are promoted', says Ricardo Semler, chief shareholder and guiding light of these changes. His success at Semco has led to him being voted Brazilian Businessman of the Year – twice.

This emphatic commitment to empowerment has brought international acclaim as well as real commercial success to Semco. It could do the same for your organisation too.

# Index

■